CHANGES IN HARMONY

"PARTNERS IN PROGRESS" BY NEISHA CHASE

Produced in cooperation with the
Yuba County-Sutter County Regional Arts Council

Windsor Publications, Inc.
Northridge, California

CHANGES IN HARMONY

AN ILLUSTRATED HISTORY OF YUBA AND SUTTER COUNTIES

MARJORIE GORDON

Previous page: Cattle still range the Loma Rica foothills of Yuba County. This painting depicts a familiar seasonal scene, ''Autumn Drive.'' Painting by Keith Christie

This book
is dedicated, respectfully,
to teachers.

**Windsor Publications, Inc.
History Books Division**

Managing Editor Karen Story
Design Director Alexander D'Anca

Staff for *Changes in Harmony: An Illustrated History of Yuba and Sutter Counties*

Development Editor Jerry Mosher
Manuscript Editor Amy Adelstein
Photo Editor Lynne Ferguson Chapman
Production Editor Robin Mastrogeorge
Editor, Corporate Biographies Brenda Berryhill
Production Editor, Corporate Biographies Thelma Fleischer
Senior Proofreader Susan J. Muhler
Editorial Assistants Didier Beauvoir,
Rebecca Kropp,
Kim Kievman,
Michael Nugwynne,
Kathy B. Peyser,
Pat Pittman,
Theresa Solis
Sales Representatives, Corporate Biographies Clair Freeman,
Gina Woolf
Layout Artist, Corporate Biographies Mari Catherine Preimesberger
Designer Thomas Prager

Library of Congress Catalog-in-Publication Data

Gordon, Marjorie.
    Changes in harmony: an illustrated history of Yuba and Sutter counties.
    Bibliography: p. 123
    Includes index.
    1. Yuba County (Calif.)—History. 2. Yuba County (Calif.)—Description and travel—Views. 3. Yuba County (Calif.)—Industries. 4. Sutter County (Calif.)—History. 5. Sutter County (Calif.)—Description and travel—Views. 6. Sutter County (Calif.)—Industries. I. Title.
F868.Y8G66 1988   979.4'34—dc19   88-14844
ISBN: 0-89781-232-8

||||||

Windsor Publications, Inc.
Elliot Martin, Chairman of the Board
James L. Fish, III, Chief Operating Officer
Hal Silverman, Vice President/Publisher

CONTENTS

P.W. Griffiths, Marysville photographer, posed his subjects, A.M. Hewitt and his daughter Inez, on a bicycle in this 1890 portrait. Courtesy, Special Collections, Meriam Library, California State University, Chico, and Sutter County Community Memorial Museum

A cow ruminates in the Sutter Buttes. Photo by Walt Anderson

PREFACE

The way to study the past is not to confine oneself to mere knowledge of history but, through application of this knowledge, to give actuality to the past.
—*I Ching*

Fortunately for writers, historians have already searched the archives and pondered the secrets therein. It is historians who, having read the diaries, letters, and documents, record and compare the evidence.

Conflicting statements arise; for example, a police report does not agree with the defense testimony. Neither public figures nor private citizens willingly divulge errors of judgment. Dreams often invade reality. Speculations fill gaps in documentation. Indeed, facts are negotiable.

With this in mind I settled upon an approach to writing which acknowledges that although elements of fiction enter into the history, if you don't tell the truth, nobody will read your book. I have occasionally made personal choices about veracity from among conflicting records. I hope the results are convincing.

The fourth annual Dove Stew outing of the Yuba and Sutter Gun Club took place at Shelton's Grove in Marysville on July 31, 1898. Three thousand doves plus venison and ''floppers'' (ducks) served 1,500 men. Gambling paid for the food, liquor, and prizes, and led to such riotous revelry that prominent women eventually succeeded in disbanding the club. Photo by C.R. Burleson. Courtesy, Special Collections, Meriam Library, California State University, Chico

ACKNOWLEDGMENTS

No one accomplishes anything alone. This project was blessed at the outset by Professor Joseph A. McGowan, who, politely and irretrievably, shot my original prospectus full of holes. He and Yuba County Historian Earl Ramey saved me weeks of chasing down blind alleys in search of verification for inaccuracies. Dr. McGowan also turned over valuable files, books, and documents.

Other friends, scholars, and librarians made their collections available. Books, manuscripts, pictures, and holographs began pouring into my net. Maybelle Arnold turned over her entire California history library; curator Danae Stewart at the Mary Aaron Museum searched out books and artifacts; historian Anita Laney provided manuscripts and information; Robert Holmes made available his collection of histories and photos; and Jim Lague and other members of the Yuba-Feather Historical Association did the same, and added tours of their museum at Forbestown.

William A. Jones, head of Special Collections at the Meriam Library, California State University at Chico, and his staff provided extensive assistance and materials. The volunteers and administrators at the Sacramento History Center offered well-organized resources; personnel in the California Room of California State Library searched out important files; the Yuba County Library staff made their California Room treasures available. Chief among these are the extensive files organized by Earl Ramey over years of volunteering his research skills in Marysville's old Packard Library. Sutter County Library and the Sutter Community Memorial Museum extended research assistance, and Sacramento History Division archivists allowed the use of certain important photographs.

Early on, Candace Head, with her rare gifts of efficiency and imagination, entered the project as research assistant.

Not all contributors appeared on the scene by designation. Indeed, the anonymous gift long ago of a word processor was propitious. An improbable meeting with Dr. Oscar Lemer, an art historian, led to resolution of a major dilemma and to significant additional resources.

Another surprise opportunity was an airflight overview of Yuba and Sutter counties. Jay Border loaned his Cessna 182, and Colonel Sidney Head, A.F. Retired, piloted as well as arranged permission to fly over restricted areas.

Where professional historians left off, editor and history buff Jo Ann Anglin critiqued my manuscript. I am deeply indebted to this friend, who also serves as public information officer of the California Arts Council.

The local branch of that body, the Yuba County-Sutter County Regional Arts Council (YSRAC), sponsored this book and made its production possible. YSRAC Director Lee Burrows spread her wings over the project and its workers at the outset. Lee Burrows exemplifies the core of human benefactors who inform and enlighten the people around them. The entire Yuba-Sutter population—not least the author—is indebted to her as well as to other visionaries at the YSRAC.

CHAPTER I

PRELUDE TO HISTORY

California land formed over a period of 40 to 50 million years of continuing tectonic activity. Residues of erosion from gravity, wind, meteorites, sun, and torrential rains crept west from the Rocky Mountains into the waters beyond, accumulating to a depth of 3,000 to 4,000 feet in a broad slope from the Rockies to the Pacific Ocean.

About 10 million years ago, as a result of tectonic plate movement, the western edge of the American continent began lifting to form the Sierra Nevada. Further west, at about the same time, the Pacific plate folded in to shape the coastal mountains. Together the two ranges, which ran north and south about 400 miles at a breadth of 50 miles, outline the great central valley of California.

Sheltered between mountains, this extensive drainage plain lay unmarked, except for occasional encroachment by the sea, until some 1.9 million years ago.

Then the earth in the north valley began to crack, and molten magma bulged upward to disrupt a 30.3-square-mile circle, about 10 miles across. From

In October 1841, U.S. explorers led by Charles Wilkes camped alongside Butte Creek, east of the Sutter Buttes. A sketch by expedition artist A.T. Agate provided the details for this engraving by B.W. Shields. Courtesy, Special Collections, Meriam Library, California State University, Chico

RED CLOUD'S SONG.

[Heard by the mother of Oan-koi'-tu-peh.]

Yang-wi'-a-kan-u mai'-dum-ni.
I am the Red Cloud.
Hi-pi-ning' koi-o-di' nik bai'-shum yan'-u-nom mai'-dum-ni.
My father formed me out of the sky.
Lu'-lūl yan'-dih oi'-yih nai.
I sing [among] the mountain flowers.
Yi'-wi yan'-dih oi'-yih nai.
I sing [among] the flowering chamize of the mountains.
Wēk'-wēk yan'-dih ci'-yih nai.
I sing in the mountains [like] the *wēk'-wēk*.
Wēk'-wēk o'-di so'-lin nai.
I sing [among] the rocks [like] the *wēk'-wēk*.
Lai'-dam yan'-dih we'-we nai.
In the morning I cry in the mountains.
Lai'-dam bo u'-ye nai.
In the morning I walk the path.
Lai'-dam lūl'-luh we'-we nai.
I cry [to] the morning stars.

This sacred song, translated to English by "modern" Indians of the 1870s, was originally performed in a Maidu Indian assembly house. Courtesy, Special Collections, Meriam Library, California State University, Chico

this volcanic turbulence, sedimentary layers of earth upended to form a crater. Lacking was the expulsion of fluid igneous material necessary to create a true volcano. What emerged instead was hot, viscous andesite, reddish but otherwise similar in composition to the granite of the Rockies.

When the resulting buttes were about half a million years old, the crater burst into activity, spewing andesite and volcanic ash over a range of six miles. The sides folded in, and the remaining configuration gradually filled with sediment over the next 1.5 million years.

Today this miniature mountain range thrusts upward about 2,100 feet in Sutter County. Rich in natural gas and, seasonally, fluid with streams, once the home of golden eagles, elk, and bear, the buttes remain a compelling feature of the valley landscape.

Maidu Indian tribes began arriving in the northern Sierra foothills approximately 30,000 years ago. They lived in harmony with the flora and fauna of the north valley and the foothills and established permanent dwellings.

Indian legend describes a great flood in the distant past and formation of the earth from a dirt ball under the direction of Earth Maker, or the Great Spirit. Once the dirt ball had grown to

the size of the earth, animals persuaded Earth Maker of the value of light from the sun, moon, and stars. Earth Maker then created human beings of different colors to people all the countries of the world and to provide himself with companionship. According to the oral heritage of the Maidu tribe:

The Great Spirit worked very hard to fashion the mighty Sierra. He placed snow on the peaks, rivers in the canyons, grass in the meadows, deer in the forests, fish in the streams. Birds and flowers he made in quantities. The Great Spirit was pleased with his handiwork but suddenly realized a Coast Range was needed in the West to keep out the Big Water and to protect the valley in between.

Weary from his labors, the Great [Spirit] Father hurried toward the setting sun, carrying the remains of earth, animals, fowl and plants with him. In the center of the valley he spilled some of his burden and "Histum Yani" [the Sutter Buttes] was formed.

Another legend, borne out in part by geological records, tells of the Big Water entering the valley. Indians drowned, and all but two of them were devoured by frogs and salmon. The Great Man, Kodo-yam-peh, gave these two survivors the gift of fertility and from them came many tribes. Eventually a great Maidu chief emerged.

He [the chief] looked over the wide water and knew the fertile plains which lay underneath. For nine sleeps he lay wondering about the water. Then he commanded the Great Man to let the water flow off. Kodo-yam-peh rent open the mountains to the west and the water flowed into the Big Water.

The northwestern tribe of Maidu Indians, the Konkow, inhabited the region where the Sutter Buttes lie. Natural

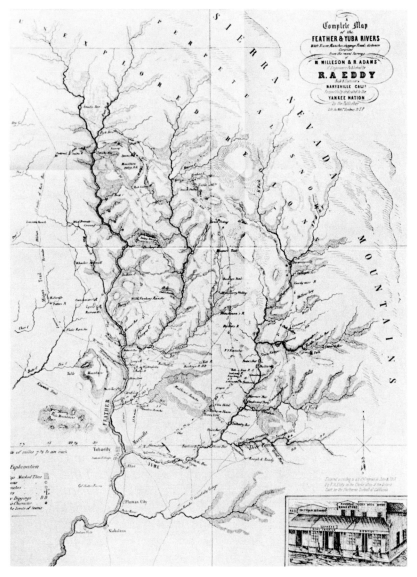

The Yuba River and Feather River territory of the Maidu Indians was mapped in 1851 and included the trails followed by white immigrants, shown as dotted lines. The Butte Mountains are in the lower left. Photo from Ramey, *The Beginnings of Marysville*, 1936. Courtesy, Special Collections, Meriam Library, California State University, Chico

drainage defined tribal territory between the Sacramento River and the Sierra Nevada.

According to historian H.H. Bancroft, writing in 1874, the Maidu generally grew to a height of 5 feet 8 inches and were dark skinned with matted black hair, cut short. Other observers noted plump bodies, strong white teeth, benign expressions, and long hair tied back in a conical shape, resembling a feather duster.

Ornamentation for men included tattoos in the form of a necklace, red or black face, and body paint. Bird bones or wood pieces were thrust through the earlobes. Women wore facial tattoos, which spread upwards from the edges of their lips to the corner of their eyes and downwards to the hinges of their jaws.

Men went naked during the hot summers. Women wore shell necklaces and summer aprons of tule grass. A mud body covering protected each Indian against the winter wind. Colder weather introduced animal-skin shawls or feather ropes wound about bodies for warmth.

Villages were comprised of blood-relative groups. Scatterings of families occupied a given tract of land which surrounded the more permanent site of a main village.

Homes were cut into the ground to a depth of 3 feet and measured 10 to 30 feet in diameter. Willow poles were driven in against the bank and bent to form circular canopies with smoke holes in the center. Mud or sod covered the dwellings, and sometimes bushes were interwoven with the poles. These more substantial structures could be used as sweat houses.

The natural environment provided plentiful grain, fish, waterfowl, grass-

Above: Indian culture is preserved and honored by Maidu descendants. Their baskets are still woven of willow and redbud, and acorns are still a staple of their diet. Photo by Walt Anderson

Right: Tufted poppies cascade over the Sutter Buttes among volcanic rock outcroppings in early springtime. Photo by Walt Anderson

Above: Only the women of the north valley Konkow tribe wore facial tattoos. Men wore paint and tattoos on other parts of the body. This drawing depicts a female Konkow, circa 1841. Courtesy, Special Collections, Meriam Library, California State University, Chico

Above: Indians dance a fandango against a background of the *Histum Yani,* or Sutter Buttes, in this 1854 drawing by Charles Nahl. From *Hutching's California Scenes,* 1855

Above: This interior view of a Maidu Indian hut, circa 1854, shows one family member repairing a fishnet and another cooking. Hunting decoys and baskets of varying sizes are scattered about. From Kroeber, *Drawn from Life: California Indians in Pen and Brush,* 1977

Above: Grasshoppers were considered a valuable food item by Maidu Indians. This crop has been chased to a trap for harvest. From *Hutching's California Magazine,* circa 1862

Above and left: Indians used baskets for carrying, cooking, eating, trapping fish, storing goods, and burying their dead. These coiled examples were made by Maidu Indians around 1889. From Heizer, *Handbook of North American Indians,* Volume 8, 1978. Courtesy, Special Collections, Meriam Library, California State University, Chico

hoppers, worms, fresh clover, and wild game. Acorns, the fruit of the giant valley oaks, were a dietary staple. Ground in rock mortars, acorn meal was leached with hot water and made into soup, bread, pudding, or mush. A single family consumed an estimated 1,000 to 2,000 pounds of acorns a year.

The abundance so freely distributed among members of the Indian cultures was believed to be granted them by departed spirits. Such beneficence prompted major gatherings and celebrations among Native Americans to honor deceased relatives.

Tribal gatherings took place yearly at traditional burning grounds, usually in autumn. The time and place were designated by the configuration of the bead strings delivered by courier to participating tribal groups.

Mourners prepared the ancestors for the gatherings by treating their graves with tears, flour, and earth a day ahead of each event. Poles were set in the ground above the burning place, and gifts were suspended on them until dawn, when they were thrown into the fire.

The likenesses of certain prominent men and women were formed into sacred images by family members. Designed to be burned, these were made of fur, bones, and feathers and then stuffed with grass. Dancing, gambling, or hand clapping were prohibited during the burning of an image, an event held sacred. Food and clothing for use in the other world could also be tossed into the fire.

While such ceremonies were taking place along the rivers and foothills of Mexican territory in the Far West, Europe and the United States were discovering industry, technology, and marketing—and cultivating greed.

European fashion dictated adornment with quantities of luxuriant furs of the sort hitherto worn by beaver, otter, fox, and mink. To meet these needs,

Hudson's Bay Company trappers ranged across North America into California. Russian traders hunted along the Pacific Coast from a base established at Fort Ross.

Captain Jedediah Smith's lucrative visit to the Konkow territory in 1827 brought more Hudson's Bay Company trappers. One of them, Michel Laframboise, entered into rites of matrimony, often with a daughter of the chief, in every Indian village he visited. Laframboise and fellow trapper John Work wintered in the "Prairie Buttes" during the floods of 1833.

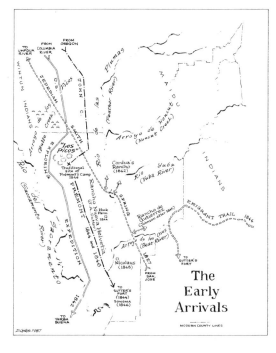

United States expeditionary forces traveled the Mexican-controlled Yuba/Sutter region before the California Gold Rush. This map, drawn by David Giles, shows the traffic that passed through the area during its last decade as wilderness.

Another trapper, Colonel J.J. Warner, described the Indians he encountered during his 1832 expedition. His second paragraph chronicles the decimation of indigenous populations by the whites' diseases:

The banks of the Sacramento River, in its whole course through its valley, were studded with Indian villages, the houses of which were red with the salmon the aborigines were curing. On no part of the continent over which I traveled was so numerous an Indian population, subsisting upon the natural products of the soil and waters.

On our return, late in the summer of 1833, we found the valleys depopulated. From the head of the Sacramento to the great bend and slough of the San Joaquin, we did not see more than six or eight live Indians, while the large numbers of their skulls and dead bodies were to be seen under almost every shade tree.

Symptoms detailed by the surviving Indians suggest that the cause of the devastation was smallpox.

In 1834 an adventurer of Swiss parentage, Captain John Augustus Sutter (born Johann August Suter), abandoned home, family, and debts for America. While engaged in trade along the Santa Fe trail, he heard tantalizing reports about land in California and, in July 1839, arrived by a circuitous route from Vancouver via the Sandwich Islands (Hawaii). Sutter immediately petitioned the Mexican government for a land grant and by August had begun con-

Confinement of the valley Indian population to rancherias resulted from expanding white settlement and agricultural use of the land. Sutter's Hock Farm was the site of this group of huts in the late 1840s. Courtesy, Special Collections, Meriam Library, California State University, Chico

This drawing portrays a Maidu Indian village on the rancheria at Hock Farm in Sutter County, circa 1840. Courtesy, Eleanor McClatchy Collection, Sacramento Museum and History Division

struction of a house on territory he named New Helvetia.

A land grant was limited to 11 leagues by Mexican decree. Sutter, however, mapped out a claim which extended well beyond this. It included some 77 leagues, which covered the territory now comprising much of Sacramento, Placer, and Nevada counties, the flatlands of Yuba County, all of Sutter County, and a fragment of Colusa. Construction of Sutter's Fort at New Helvetia began in 1841.

White settlement quickly followed, with Sutter officiating as California's first land developer. He leased and later sold land east of the Feather River, where it joined the Yuba River, to Theodor Cordua. Cordua's Ranch and trading post eventually became Marysville.

Across the Feather River, Sutter authorized General John Bidwell to establish Hock Farm as a cattle ranch. After his fort at Sacramento was pillaged by gold seekers in 1849, Sutter made Hock Farm his primary residence.

Trapper Nicolaus Altgeier arrived in 1839 and helped build the first adobe structure at Hock Farm. He received land along the Feather River that became the town of Nicolaus and there established a two-story adobe hotel. He also built a ferry, operated by Indian employees, across the river to Hock Farm.

On May 13, 1846, U.S. President James K. Polk declared war against Mex-

ico in an effort to claim California as U.S. territory. A modest altercation resulted, alienating the principal white settlers from their Mexican neighbors.

Confusion was added by Lieutenant John C. Fremont's pretensions as protector of the white settlers. Confirmed neither as hero, pathfinder, nor protector except by his own promotional efforts, Fremont nonetheless found supporters, among them the colorful frontier guide Christopher (Kit) Carson.

When he competed for the office of governor at the close of the California conquest, Fremont's army tenure outranked that of General Stephen Watts Kearny. Fremont did not assume the governorship for long, however. In fact, he was later court-martialed and stripped of rank for mutiny, disorderly conduct, and disobedience. He nonetheless went on to become the U.S. senator from California from 1850 to 1851 and the Republican candidate for president in 1856. A question remains as to whether Fremont qualifies historically for heroism or notoriety.

As California's indigenous population dwindled, glowing reports of free, rich farmland for settlement spread throughout overcrowded and industrialized Europe. Passage to America was booked by Swiss, French, German, and other European adventurers.

By 1840 nearly 40,000 Americans from the East Coast had swarmed west as far as Missouri, seeking relief from the bitter depression of the late 1830s. In 1841 the first wagon train left Independence, Missouri, to follow the Oregon Trail, which had been mapped by the Lewis and Clark expedition of 1804 to 1806.

The arrival of white settlers with livestock and ambitions for farmland redefined Indian tribal territory as real estate. Indian burial sites, homes, and food reserves all vanished into homesteads and rangeland under white control. This possession by whites of hunting, fishing,

Artist J. Ross Browne titled this circa 1864 drawing ''Protecting the Settlers''—which, for many whites, meant shooting Indians. Courtesy, Special Collections, Meriam Library, California State University, Chico

and food-gathering regions resulted in the disruption of an ecological balance of many centuries' duration. Gradual starvation nearly completed the genocide of the tribes, initiated by smallpox.

Indian reprisals took the form of raids on livestock and occasionally on homesteads. Attacks, announced beforehand by war-like shouts in the night, were usually thwarted, however. Frontier justice decreed that Indians be shot without hesitation—shooting unarmed Indians, furthermore, alleviated the drudgery and boredom of frontier life.

Opening the frontier for rangeland and agriculture brought settlers who, although plucky, had modest expectations. Within a very few years, however, the pastoral flavor of life on the land in Yuba and Sutter counties would give way to a widespread disregard of delicate natural balances.

CHAPTER II

FANTASIA IN GOLD

In 1803 the American Republic extended west as far as Missouri. President Thomas Jefferson was secretly negotiating with France for the purchase of Louisiana, while Great Britain was preparing to seize New Orleans from France.

Emperor Napoleon resolved the impending conflict by selling Louisiana to the Americans, simultaneously thwarting the British and enabling Jefferson to realize his vision of expanding the new democratic nation.

At that time the primary instigator of land development in Yuba and Sutter counties, as well as of much of California, was born on the German-Swiss border. Johann August Suter, the son of Johann Jakob Suter, the supervisor of a paper mill at Kandern, arrived at 5 A.M. on February 15, 1803. Some hold that when Sutter (his spelling) was but a mewling babe he was as well equipped to build a wilderness empire involving mammoth financial transactions and feats of diplomacy as he would ever be.

The son of disenfranchised rural citizens, the youth was dazzled by a pass-

Marysville superseded other ports in 1850 to become the gateway to the mines. Courtesy, The Bancroft Library

ing parade of ostentatious nobility and uniformed armies. Desiring wealth and position but denied them by a rigid social structure, Sutter became a man of grandiose mannerisms propped up by plebeian foundations. His character was rife with contradictions: he was candid although inventive; trusting yet irresponsible; highly intelligent despite a mediocre education. He taught himself to converse—ungrammatically—in several languages.

Above all the man was charming. Sutter's social success derived from an apparent respect for each individual with whom he came into contact, whether aborigine, diplomat, general, or underling—with the notable exception of members of his immediate family.

At 16 Sutter was apprenticed to a publisher and bookseller in Basel, to be discharged in 1823. He clerked for a cloth merchant, then a grocer. While so employed, on October 24, 1826, he married Anna Dubeld, a widowed merchant's daughter, who bore him his first son the following day.

Thanks to his mother-in-law's influence, Sutter bought a drygoods store and moved his family upstairs, where he lived extravagantly. The firm collapsed within three years.

Sutter's many creditors received only 25 percent settlements. Disgraced and without prospects in the Old World, the New World beckoned. The former clerk absconded, leaving behind a debt of some 35,000 francs and a warrant for his arrest.

The above details derive from historical records. Sutter himself, declaring his past to have been quite otherwise, says that he was

born of a respectable family enjoying independent circumstances. I received a good education, literary and military. I entered as cadet at Berne, Switzerland, and served in the army until I went to America in 1834. Was officer in the Swiss Army at the time of Napoleon III,

was a refugee in Switzerland and captain of artillery.

Not a word did he say about his abandoned wife and children. He also claimed to have been a classmate of Louis Napoleon, later Emperor of France, at a prestigious military academy.

Never mind, the man became so cognizant of the material he lied about, so appealing and credible, that everyone believed him. No one failed to be touched by his kindness of heart.

Sutter arrived in New York in July 1834, determined to join the ranks of landed gentry in the New World. He wintered in St. Louis and St. Charles. He emerged from an unsuccessful trading enterprise to Santa Fe with diminished funds; his partners claimed total ruin. Joining a party of explorers, he arrived at Fort Vancouver in October 1838.

Taking a roundabout route to California, he sailed for the Sandwich Islands (Hawaii). There he accumulated influential friends and bought a ship, the *Clementine*, complete with its cargo, and servants. There also he exchanged his tawdry beginnings for a fine fiction full of resplendence and grandeur, incidentally promoting himself to captain in the army of Charles X of France.

With the *Clementine's* cargo delivered to Sitka, where he made more friends and gathered additional letters of introduction from the Russian governor, Sutter sailed south to Alta California.

At Monterey, Governor Juan Bautista Alvarado read the many letters praising Sutter and granted him permission to farm 11 leagues of wilderness in the central valley. Sutter was also promised citizenship in one year.

Thus was founded, on August 13, 1839, the colony of New Helvetia. Indians opposed the landing of 4 white men and 10 Sandwich Islanders on the banks of the Sacramento River, but Sutter's charm and appreciation of ceremony soon won their allegiance. He lost no time in assuming a role of absolute

Captain John Sutter gained a stature in America unattainable in his native Switzerland. In 1855 he posed in full military regalia for former New York artist William Smith Jewett. His fort at New Helvetia is visible in the background. Photo by Page Atwater. Courtesy, Sacramento Museum and History Division

Arrival at the Sutter Buttes ended the old way of life for settlers. This engraving from *Picturesque America*, an 1850s publication, shows that the transition could be difficult for even the wealthier wagon owners. Courtesy, Eleanor McClatchy Collection, Sacramento Museum and History Division

authority, offering rewards for work and acting swiftly in punishment.

A year later Sutter became a naturalized Mexican citizen and was appointed judge and government representative for the inland territory, with what he called "power of life and death over all subjects." In June 1841 he received the land grant entitling him with ownership, as promised by Alvarado.

New Helvetia could not flourish without goods and livestock, all of which Sutter collected, with pleas and promises, from the Mexican government, U.S. Consul Thomas Larkin, and other settlers. Soap, seed corn, beans, wheat, cattle, iron, sheep, ammunition, horses, and cloth all came to Sutter's Fort in exchange for promissory fabrications. Some donors were paid at the expense of others; many simply lost out. While Sutter routinely failed to live up to his promises to donors, he rarely failed to take risks with other men's labor. The first settlers in New Helvetia were trappers, sailors who jumped ship, and other renegades. Nevertheless they were disciplined by Sutter and became a valuable workforce for the colony.

The 1830s depression, coupled with the promotion of a doctrine of "Manifest Destiny" which proclaimed the right and duty of Americans to expand the

territory and influence of the United States, catered to the longings of males more restless even than Sutter. The U.S. government had splendid, rousing terms such as "patriotism" to describe these feelings. Thus little reason remained for any man to deny his urge to move on, explore the West, and carve a home out of the wilderness. Never mind if the wife and children in most cases were left behind to fend for themselves, or else "the chattel" was told to pack up and join the tortuous trek across the continent. These men were bent on self-actualization.

By 1841 the lands as far west as Missouri were filled. New horizons beckoned still further west.

In May 1841 a 20-year-old teacher, John Bidwell, relinquished his 160 acres in Missouri without protest to a claim jumper. Underage for officially owning property, Bidwell started west with the first organized caravan. Another westward trailblazer was Nancy Kelsey, the first white woman to cross the Sierra Nevada. Kelsey, with a baby girl on one hip at the outset, is included on the frontier roster as "and wife" after the name of husband Benjamin.

At the Sierra pass now known as Sonora, the party abandoned its wagons; oxen, then mules, were consumed for food. No one dared ride horseback down the now hazardous trail to the valley. Kelsey, barefoot and exhausted, led her horse nearly to Mt. Diablo, until she collapsed near the outpost of "Dr." John Marsh and was revived with a dish of cereal.

Kelsey then followed her husband and his brother Andrew all over Northern California on trapping expeditions. The child she carried across the Sierra died six years later, scalped by Indians. Kelsey's white underskirt provided the material for the Bear Flag raised at Sonoma in 1846. Eventually the brothers gathered a million dollars in gold dust, which was soon lost and stolen.

Such intrepid pioneers scattered

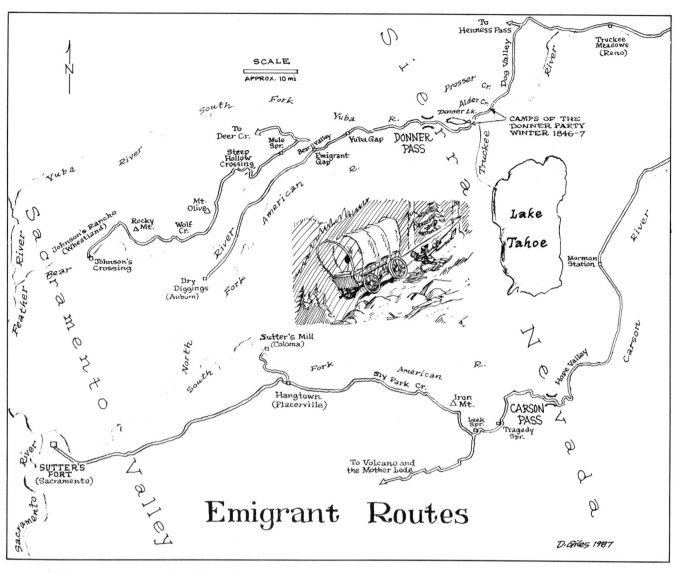

Emigrant Routes

D. Giles 1987

across California to acquire land, found families, and become revered by historians. Bidwell and the Kelseys headed north to Sutter's Fort where all were taken in by the hospitable Swiss and offered jobs.

Bidwell was employed by Sutter as chief assistant. His first job was to oversee the details of Sutter's purchase of the Russian colony at Fort Ross. Since the Russians lacked guaranteed title to the land, only livestock and equipment were negotiated in the sale. Most of these goods were transported to New Helvetia. Bidwell would become one of Sutter's few enduring and trustworthy friends.

Other Europeans sought freedom and fortune in Northern California. Until 1848, when gold was discovered, "fortune" meant fertile farmlands, winter trapping, or trading. Explorer Theodor

Cordua, for example, found the rich river bottomland of Yuba and Sutter counties appealing, and stayed.

Cordua left Germany as a young man and spent 20 years in South America before he gathered up his worldly goods and headed for the Mexican land of California to the north. He landed in Monterey and then in 1842 sailed up the Sacramento River to Captain Sutter's New Helvetia.

Cordua exchanged his cargo, valued at $8,000, for a 19-year lease on all of Sutter's holdings north of the Yuba River. A promise by Sutter to supply hogs, cattle, oxen, and horses concluded the bargain. Cordua petitioned the Mexican government for another seven leagues to the north and east, which were granted him in December 1844 by Mexican governor Manuel Micheltorena. Cordua's holdings thus covered the ter-

Settlers choosing to travel on the California Trail left the Oregon Trail at Snake River and followed the Humboldt River through Utah. They crossed the Sierra Nevada at Carson and Donner passes to reach Sacramento Valley settlements. Map by David Giles

Because the mountains were already impassable in November of 1846, the hapless Donner Party built cabins and prepared for the winter. Courtesy, Mary Aaron Museum

ritory now known as Marysville, which extended north to the Feather River and Honcut Creek, south to the Yuba River, and east to the Sierra foothills.

Indian residents were included in land grants as the new owner's subjects. Cordua was unique in treating the Native Americans with dignity and giving them payment for their services. A benevolent despotism reigned until later settlers adopted a confrontational stance toward the indigenous tribes.

The U.S. government encouraged the appropriation of California from Mexico. A thwarted Bear Flag Revolt took place at Sonoma on June 14, 1846, when Captains Ezekiel Merritt and William B. Ide seized the settlement and hoisted a man-made "bear" flag. A few weeks later Commodore John D. Sloat's forces took the Mexican presidio at Monterey. By July 11, U.S. flags flew at Monterey, Yerba Buena (San Francisco), Sonoma, Bodega, and New Helvetia.

The Revolt lasted two years, until September 14, 1847, with most of the action taking place in the southern part

of the territory. The Treaty of Guadalupe Hidalgo, signed on February 2, 1848, and ratified on May 30, ceded California to the United States.

Pioneers following the Oregon Trail had meanwhile trickled into California's central valley. Others had crossed the northern Sierra Nevada, with varying success. One party, led by George Donner, attempted the precipitous mountain crossing from Truckee in October 1846.

That year, prolonged winter snows struck the Sierra Nevada a month earlier than anticipated, and with brutal and unremitting force. The Donner party halted at a lake near Truckee, unable to proceed or retreat. While they awaited rescue, their draft animals either succumbed to avalanches or were eaten.

In December 17 members of the party headed west in search of help. After 32 days and 90 miles, seven barely alive stragglers reached the Bear River ranch of William Johnson. After another 10 days relief was dispatched from Sutter's Fort to the remnant still in the mountains. Their struggle for life in the

grip of storms, disease, and starvation continued until a fourth and final relief party rescued the last survivor in April 1847.

Of the original 90 members of the Donner party, 48 remained alive. A few settled at Cordua's Ranch.

Thereafter, land emigration continued across the Sierra Nevada to the north and south. After the Donner casualties, travel near Donner Pass, as the crossing became known, was rare.

Meanwhile, with the help of peaceable workers, Cordua constructed an adobe home and other buildings at the confluence of the Yuba and Feather rivers. The soil was tilled and planted, and his animal herds increased.

The next logical development was to market the abundant produce to oncoming pioneers. Cordua's Ranch, as the trading post became known, began in the original adobe house alongside the Yuba River at what is now the foot of D Street.

In 1847 Cordua employed up to 20 Europeans and Indians. His ranch held thousands of cattle and hundreds of horses. Trading expanded by boat between Cordua's Ranch and Yerba Buena, a forerunner of San Francisco.

West across the Feather River John Bidwell accepted the job of managing Captain Sutter's New Helvetia property, Hock Farm. The land had supported the largest of Sutter County's Indian villages, the Hocks, which numbered from 80 to 100 inhabitants. Bidwell established a home, orchards, and a garden and took charge of the 5,000 head of cattle and 1,200 horses ranging Sutter's land between the Feather and Sacramento rivers.

The fertile river valley, which boasted wild grains reaching as high as a man's shoulders, an abundance of game birds and fish, wood for fuel, and river transport, was viewed as a paradise by entrepreneurs.

Left unexploited by the native population for 30,000 years, the land was ripe for development. The possession of rich land in unlimited quantities was the prize and pride of the early settlers, the

One of the rescue parties dispatched by Captain John Sutter from New Helvetia, in February 1847, was eagerly welcomed by Donner Party survivors. Courtesy, Mary Aaron Museum

A French mining company proposed mechanical exploration of the California mines and rivers; this poster, circa 1850, gives the details of the proposal. From Pennoyer, *This Was California*, 1938. Courtesy, Special Collections, Meriam Library, California State University, Chico

From Hallwood in the valley, Stamfield Hill is visible above the Loma Rica foothills. Situated on the Marysville/Camptonville Road, this 640-acre ranch and hotel, including a stage stop, was built by Stamfield and taken over by Charles Smith in 1858. Courtesy, Maybelle Arnold

realization of their dreams.

At this pinnacle of prosperity, a new sawmill of Sutter's at Coloma yielded an unforeseen fringe benefit: gold. Having discovered this, sawmill foreman John Marshall dropped everything and, with a pea-sized nugget and some dust, rode off to Sutter at New Helvetia.

Theodor Cordua happened by Sutter's Fort on a business trip. "Unimpressive," Cordua wrote in his journal, ignorant of the effect Marshall's discovery would have on his Yuba River paradise. Cordua proceeded on to Yerba Buena, more mindful of hay trading.

It took the promotional efforts of Sam Brannan, entrepreneur, merchant, Mormon, and newspaper editor, to spread the gold fever. First Brannan the merchant bought up supplies for his store at Sacramento, then Brannan the editor traveled to Yerba Buena and, in a frenzy of enthusiasm, began shouting "Gold in California!"

Get rich quick; just dip a pan in a California river and untold wealth is yours. All you need is a pick, a pan, and a shovel, conveniently stocked by Sam Brannan at Sacramento.

Cordua's hay loaders heard the call and vanished. The trader salvaged what he could, accepted his losses, and headed back north to what he assumed to be a safe haven at the Yuba River. Many of Yerba Buena's adventurers passed him along the way, bent on riches.

When he returned, Cordua found that his ranch had been abandoned. Greed had overcome his trusted employees. They had left his herds untended, his crops unharvested, and his home dismantled. Former employees and newcomers alike were already situated along creekbeds throughout the foothills, mining with equipment fashioned from pillaged floorboards of Cordua's and others' homes and nourishing themselves with pilfered rations.

A French barrelmaker by the name of Charles Covillaud, who had worked for Cordua since 1846, was one of the

fortunate few who found rich diggings. Covillaud's success allowed him to return to his former employer and purchase a half interest in the depleted property for $12,500.

During the 10-year heyday of Fort Sutter which ended with the Gold Rush, Sutter provided rest, jobs, and services to virtually all the Northern California settlers. He established workshops, mills, a distillery, a tannery, a blacksmith, a bakery, and other necessities of frontier development. A unique accomplishment was Sutter's small, mostly Indian army of trained and uniformed soldiers.

The visions of grandeur and social distinction, which once drove the insignificant Swiss clerk to overextend credit, materialized for him in California. Sutter, however, lacked managerial skills, and both his high-spirited entertainments and extravagant humanitarian missions disrupted the beaver-pelt trade as much as they had European banking. No request for assistance went unheeded. Search and rescue parties for distressed pioneers left Sutter's Fort regularly, often accompanied by Sutter himself.

New Helvetia had reached its peak

of prosperity in 1848 with the construction of grist mills and sawmills. Sutter was obligated by the Fort Ross agreement to ship large amounts of foodstuffs to the Russian colony at Sitka. He promised his creditors the mill could grind all the wheat produced in the valley. The mill at Coloma would provide all the lumber necessary. The plan seemed feasible until fate intervened with foreman John Marshall's discovery.

Gold seekers, charlatans, and carousers descended greedily upon the established settlement. They plundered equipment and livestock from Fort Sutter. Soon the timbers of both mills disappeared into the gold fields.

Now Sutter received word that his eldest son, Johann August, Jr., had left Switzerland and was bound for California. The Russians were demanding payment in cash and produce for Fort Ross, on which Sutter had defaulted for three years. One grain crop had failed during the Mexican War campaign, and the fields had been left untended as all his employees had deserted to the diggings. Only a group of Mormons remained, briefly, out of respect for the hospitality

Whaleboats transported miners upriver to the gold diggings. This view of the upper Sacramento was drawn by Jules Tavernier in 1877. From Kroeber, *Drawn from Life: California Indians in Pen and Brush,* 1977. Courtesy, Special Collections, Meriam Library, California State University, Chico

the moment.

Sutter next received notice of the arrival of his wife, two other sons, and a daughter, Eliza, at San Francisco.

The unbidden Sutter family settled in at Hock Farm. They were joined by Sutter, Jr., when debts were cleared at Sutterville and the power of attorney returned to his father. Sutter's future choices of agents excluded his capable son.

Hock Farm meanwhile became the setting for lavish parties. Boatloads of revelers, musicians, fine wines, and free-

they had received.

Threatened with losing everything, Sutter relinquished the title of New Helvetia to his son, who sold enough land to cover his father's most pressing obligations. Sutter, rescued from the brink, nonetheless assailed his son and savior and, embittered by his losses, moved to his haven alongside the Feather River. Hock Farm thus became the foundation of Sutter County.

Under Bidwell's prudent management the property now consisted of a fine home with extensive orchards and range land. It was safe from creditors for

loaders descended upon the famous host. Wife Anna, however, did not participate in revelry of any sort.

Between parties Sutter sent abroad for cuttings and seeds and experimented with plantings. The resulting stock formed the nucleus of the extensive orchards, gardens, and grainfields which today support Sutter County's prosperity.

The Sutter offspring, who had been raised in privation by their mother, now understood their father to be the richest man in California and acted accordingly. Yet, full of resentment and lacking their father's grace and courtliness, they were perceived by neighbors and visitors as rude, boorish, and conceited.

Within half a year the family fortune vanished again due to Sutter's extravagance. Moreover, rustlers pillaged his cattle; squatters stole his fruit and cut down his beloved forests of oak and sycamore. Agents squirreled away large commissions from simultaneous sales of the same property to different buyers, with interest running at 10 percent per month. One $5,000 debt rose to $35,000 before Sutter learned of the transaction.

Eventually all the servants were let go, and the younger generation of Sutters learned the value of labor, with the three boys in the fields and Eliza in the kitchen.

Across the Feather River gold fever was rendering men delirious. South Americans sailed up the Pacific Coast. Fortune seekers from the East Coast of the U.S. arrived by wagon, sailed around Cape Horn, or trekked by mule or by foot across the Isthmus of Panama and reembarked northward to California. Overpopulated European nations loaded their excess population onto westbound ships. Within two years 80,000 newcomers had poured into the gold country.

Gamblers, thieves, and assorted other scoundrels came to California along with honest laborers, settlers, and miners. Cards and liquor became as vital to the lonely argonaut as his pick and pan. For recreation after a strenuous day's labor or celebration after a profit-

Scenes from a day in the life of a northern California miner during the 1850s are depicted here. Courtesy, The Bancroft Library

During the gold mining days, the laborers of every ethnic group, including these Chinese, entertained themselves by gambling. Note the artist's emphasis on slanted eyes and sinister facial expressions. The scene by the river may have been Celestial Valley, near Camptonville on Oregon Creek, where 500 Chinese miners worked. Courtesy, The Bancroft Library

MINERS

GAMBLERS

able strike, for solace over loneliness or disapppointment, or as tonic during illness, a bottle of whiskey was mandatory and ensured camaraderie.

Next a contingent of hoteliers, merchants, teamsters, mesdames, and physicians arrived to offer their services.

Dame Shirley Clapp accompanied her physician husband up the Feather River to Rich Bar in 1851 and recorded the details of life in a mining camp with wit and perception:

Whether there is more profanity in the mines than elsewhere, I know not; but during the short time that I have been at Rich Bar, I have heard more of it than in all my life before. Of course, the most vulgar blackguard will abstain from swearing in the presence of a lady; but in this rag and card-board house, one is compelled to hear the most sacred of names constantly profaned by the drinkers and gamblers who haunt the barroom at all hours.

Some of these expressions, were they not so fearfully blasphemous, would be grotesquely sublime. For instance; not five minutes ago, I heard two men quarrelling in the street, and one said to the other, "only let me get hold of your beggarly carcass once, and I will use you up so small that God Almighty himself cannot see your ghost!"

Such colloquy entertained the North Americans so thoroughly that the formal English of "foreigners" was held in contempt. Attempts on the part of French, East Indian, Chilean, Mexican, German, and Chinese immigrants to understand or be understood through conventional study of the rules of English grammar failed utterly. Besides, the "Americans" had "got there first."

Mob strength and white supremacy ruled. The customary behavior of "foreigners," deemed courteous in their own cultures, was perceived by boisterous Yankees as decidedly unfriendly. "Somehow, they ain't folksy!" chimed

the more moderate.

A strict hierarchy evolved, with American hotheads, whose roots went back less than a generation or two, on top. Newly arrived, light-skinned Caucasians, especially rich ones, were accepted at high levels of society. Bigotry was evident, however, against dark-complexioned Spaniards. The dusky Sandwich Island Kanakas were barely acknowledged as human, and Indians suffered severely diminished rights in their own territory. Relegated to the bottom of the heap, contemptible even to the misprized Indians, were the Chinese, with no legal or social rights whatsoever.

Status in society was thus based almost entirely on two criteria: facility with the American language and skin color. Education, expertise, culture, aristocracy, or intelligence did not signify if the possessor had dark or yellow skin; even wealth held no power in a society where thievery reigned.

Flagrant examples of bigotry, lawlessness, and greed were yet counter-

During the Gold Rush days, a tax of $20 per month was levied on "foreign miners." Here the Indians collect from a group of Chinese miners, having learned new manners from the white man. Courtesy, Special Collections, Meriam Library, California State University, Chico

Originally settled by Henry Reed in 1850, the former Reed's Station was deeded to Daniel A. Ostrom in 1873. Six miles north of Johnson's Crossing, the station made large yearly shipments of grain by rail. Courtesy, Maybelle Arnold

balanced by moments of gentleness, wisdom, and hospitality. And unperturbed by this human drama, nature's great levelers—floods, fires, droughts, blizzards—continued to operate.

Rites of passage among the gold seekers, which involved confronting unimaginable deprivation, loneliness, failure, and despair, as well as other experiences designed to illustrate the folly of greed or to cause premature demise, were known as "seeing the elephant." Few prospectors failed to "see the elephant"; indeed many had a good look while still crossing the plains.

Meanwhile, the process of extracting abundance from the bountiful land—which meant "civilization"—continued, invigorated by the massive influx of gold seekers and settlers.

In 1849 Sam Brannan and Shasta County rancher Pierson B. Reading negotiated with Sutter for the purchase of two leagues of land west of the Feather River. They developed the $2,000 purchase into the town of Yuba City across from Cordua's Ranch. Reading and surveyor Joseph Ruth laid out a city in blocks and squares, leveling Indian burial mounds on the site. Within a year Yuba City boasted 150 settlers, over 20 stores, and a ferry that operated between the town and Marysville.

The flood of 1849, which had dis-

suaded a young attorney, Stephen J. Field, from locating his practice at Vernon, opened river traffic as far north as Yuba City and Marysville.

A legislative body for the California territory had convened in San Jose on December 15, 1849. By February 1850, boundaries were set for 27 counties. Yuba County included the present Nevada County and part of Placer County until a later reapportionment. News of California's admission to the United States arrived in October 1850.

Marysville, on the side of the gold-bearing foothills, parlayed the blessings of nature into status over Yuba City as "The Queen City of the North," despite

major efforts by Sutter County promoters. Many of Yuba City's founders uprooted themselves and relocated across the river to share in Marysville's prosperity. Enjoying prominence for the next decade or two, Marysville merchants filled the daily pack trains to the mines. As a boisterous, prospering gateway to the mines, Marysville flourished as a major commercial center north of San Francisco.

In 1852 new settlers began farming the rich bottomlands of Sutter County. Soon bridges connected the two rival towns, and the groundwork was established for Yuba City's future preeminence in agriculture.

Above: D Street in Marysville developed as a major trading center, receiving goods by streamer to fill ox carts and mule trains bound for the mines upriver. Courtesy, Special Collection, Meriam Library, California State University, Chico

Top: Marysville plaza is seen from a Yuba River vantage point in 1851. Within a few months of this drawing this area was in flames. Courtesy, The Bancroft Library

CHAPTER III

ORCHESTRATING PROSPERITY

In the exuberant frontier outpost called Cordua's Ranch (Marysville), the reins of power shifted capriciously as gold fortunes beckoned and vanished. Charles Covillaud's partnership with his former employer ended abruptly and inexplicably, and in January 1848 Theodor Cordua sold the remaining portion of his once extensive ranch to a pair of brothers-in-law, Michael C. Nye and William Foster.

The property became known as Nye's Ranch. Cordua, after departing for Europe with the dregs of a fortune and his unfulfilled dreams, was dealt a further blow by being robbed during the passage.

Covillaud's new partners, Foster and Nye, were married to two sisters, Sarah and Harriet Murphy, who were survivors of the Donner tragedy. A third sister, 18-year-old Mary Murphy, became Covillaud's bride at Christmastime, 1848.

Covillaud bought out his brothers-in-law in September 1849 for $30,000. He then engaged in a partnership with Chilean entrepreneur Manuel Ramirez and John Sampson, an Englishman.

The *Governor Dana* first traveled the Feather River to Marysville in April 1850. It is shown here as it passed the Sutter County ranch of Joseph Girdner. Courtesy, Mary Aaron Museum

California's second oldest courthouse was built in 1854 in the fast-growing town of Marysville. The imposing Gothic structure was a highlight of Sacramento Valley architecture for many years, but it was demolished in 1963 along with its neighbor, the Hall of Records, built in 1860. The courthouse is shown here in 1922. Photo by Henry Sackrider. Courtesy, California State Library

Ramirez envisioned Marysville as a feudal state with himself as lord of the manor. The castle he built still stands on Fifth Street opposite the Yuba County Courthouse; but feudalism, waning in Europe since the French Revolution, failed to materialize in Marysville.

In 1849 a sailing ship entered San Francisco Bay and continued upriver to Sacramento. Several American businessmen from the East Coast had brought parts for a small stern-wheel steamer on their voyage around Cape Horn. They disembarked at Sutter's Fort, assembled the mechanism, and installed it on the small ship they christened *Linda.*

The Linda Company, as the group called itself, piloted the steamer up the Feather River to Nye's Ranch (Marysville) in December 1849. The winter-swollen Yuba carried them further east to rapids near the ranch owned by John Rose and George Kinlock.

There the Linda Company determined to establish the head of navigation to serve the mines. Rose was encouraged to lay out a town a mile square that was to be named, unremarkably, Linda. Although the town of Linda failed, the steamer *Linda* commenced biweekly runs between Sacramento and Marysville.

Frenchman Theodore Sicard, the first tenant of Sutter's Hock Farm and a settler since 1845, took his Indian "subjects" into the hills for gold and came back with $70,000. For $22,500 he too bought a share of Covillaud and Company. When land development superseded gold, the partners decided to build a town. Surveyor Augustus Le Plongeon arrived at that moment from France.

Covillaud commissioned a master plan for his town, which Le Plongeon laid out with numerous parks and open spaces. Le Plongeon considered its elegance as fitting the beauty of the landscape with its river confluences, huge, graceful oaks, and nearby mountain ranges.

New arrivals had built a tent city of 300 residents by January 15, 1850. Within a month that number swelled to 1,500: 500 permanent residents; the remainder, travelers heading up the rivers for gold. Merchants filled Yubaville's waterfront plaza, their wares spread out in boxes and on bales. Amidst the sheltering trees a lusty commerce flourished.

Meanwhile in San Francisco a young attorney, Stephen J. Field, was being urged to build his practice at Vernon, where the Sacramento and Feather rivers met. He arrived there in January 1850 aboard a small steamer, the *Lawrence,* to find "a solitary house standing in a vast lake of water." The outlook did not look propitious, and Field informed the captain he would stay on board.

The steamer followed the Feather River to Nicolaus and then to Nye's Ranch, where Field disembarked. As soon as he was ashore, he was hustled into the old Cordua Adobe and shown a map of "Yubaville." In his account he records hearing a clerk say, "Gentlemen, put your names down, all you that want lots."

"But suppose a man afterwards don't want the lots," ventured Field.

"Oh, you need not take them if you don't want them" was the reply. Field's narrative continues:

I took him at his word and wrote my name down for sixty-five lots, aggregating in all $16,250. This produced a great sensation. To the best of my recollection I had only about twenty dollars . . . but it was immediately noised about that a great capitalist had come up from San Francisco to invest in lots in the rising town.

Two of the proprietors, Covillaud and Sicard, were delighted I could speak French and insisted on showing me the town site. It was a beautiful spot, covered with live-oak trees that reminded me of the oak parks in England, and the neighborhood was lovely. I saw at once that the place, from its position at the head of practical river navigation, was destined to become an important depot, and that its beauty and salubrity would render it a pleasant place to live.

Field let his credentials be known and was quickly commissioned to draw up a proper deed to the land being sold. Sutter was summoned from Hock Farm to sign the paper, and the two men established a firm friendship.

With an orderly process of land development in place, Field then persuaded the town proprietors to follow legal procedures for recording deeds, preserving order, and settling disputes. Within three days of his arrival, he was elected to the office of alcalde, under Mexican law a position of considerable power.

At the election held in front of the original Cordua Adobe the evening of January 18, 1850, someone suggested the town have an official name. A discussion of names like Yubaville, Yubafield, and Circumdoro followed, until one prominent citizen suggested Marysville to honor the most renowned American woman of the town, Mary Covillaud. Great enthusiasm, loud hurrahs, and circling hats unanimously confirmed the new name.

No time was lost during Marysville's first year as a city. An 1850 census recorded 1,428 residents. Two riverboats, the *Lawrence* and the *Linda,* threaded their way daily through mud and snags between Sacramento and Marysville.

Pack trains and wagons carried supplies along primitive trails to the foothills. Eventually public tollroads were

Marysville was destined to become the center of navigation for mining and settlement trade because of its river access. This lithograph from 1862 shows the thriving town with river traffic and the substantial Eldorado Hotel. Courtesy, California State Library

designated wherever trail was broken, and improvements began.

A Methodist Episcopal church opened in Marysville, and a graciously appointed "Hotel for Invalids" became the first hospital. Four stage lines operated, with mail service out of Marysville's new post office. A Court of Sessions opened, and in May the first California State Legislature assigned the Eighth District Court judge to Marysville.

In an effort to welcome the new District Court judge, William R. Turner, Alcalde Field sent a treasured packet of New York newspapers to Turner's office. Among them was an issue of the *Evening Post* which Judge Turner lambasted as abolitionist. Accusing Field of abolitionist sentiments, Turner launched a bitter campaign in courtroom, newspaper, and street to discredit Field.

Among the consequences for Field were the ruin of his law practice and a considerable financial loss. The altercation also led Field to seek election to the state legislature. Once elected he established Codes of Civil and Criminal Procedure which prevented illegal and vengeful actions by District Court judges.

Field also managed to remodel the Judicial Districts so that the northern wilderness of Trinity and Klamath counties comprised Turner's new Eighth District. Sutter and Yuba counties formed Judicial District Ten.

During the course of their extensive travels, a Boston couple, Mr. and Mrs. D.B. Bates, spent three years, 1851 to 1854, in Marysville. Mrs. Bates, a keen observer, commented upon their arrival at Marysville, "The sun was just gliding over the tops of the little canvas stores

surrounding the plaza, literally swarming with people who had gathered for the landing." She found the river townsite "romantic in the extreme, with [a] thick growth of trees bestudding the banks and dipping gracefully into the smoothly gliding current; the branches uniting overhead and forming a leafy canopy."

Four first-class hotels, the United States, the Tremont, the Oriental, and the St. Charles, offered shelter, with board priced at $4 per day. Noise and confusion raged through the streets, however, limiting sleep.

News of any theater opening was announced by a town crier on horseback, galloping through the town. Saloons, a gambling house, and a bowling alley thrived. Women were scarce, children even more so.

Adding to the cacophony of a bus-

tling town were some 4,000 mules employed in pack trains to the mines.

A brick jail was constructed in 1850, and a Marysville newspaper, the *Herald*, printed its first issue in August 1850. Formation of a fire department, however, was delayed.

Marysville's first Chinese inhabitant owned and operated a laundry. A fire which broke out there in August 1851 burned down 80 buildings, nearly the entire town. This and other fires helped convince the city fathers of the need for fire protection. Not until 1857, however, did adobe and brick take precedence over wood as construction material.

As a tourist Mrs. Bates recorded that she forded the river by wagon in 1853 to visit Yuba City, which, "with the exception of three or four houses, had been removed to Marysville." She

This lithograph depicts the burning of Marysville on the night of August 30, 1851. Courtesy, The Bancroft Library

This is the view of Sutter's Hock Farm that Mrs. D.B. Bates of Boston first had from the Feather River, about 1855. Courtesy, Special Collections, Meriam Library, California State University, Chico

toured Sutter's Indian Rancheria, which regularly attracted visitors, and described the Indians as "decidedly pleasant." The babies "are beauties. Their mothers learn them to swim as an old duck does her young. They build little pens at the brink of the river and put the children in the shallow water and keep them there half the time. They are really amphibious."

The Indian women had been making bread by grinding acorns and worms, and they offered some to the visitors. Mrs. Bates politely declined.

To reach Hock Farm, Mrs. Bates followed the banks of the Feather River "until the picturesque mansion of the affable and dignified General" came into view. Here Mrs. Bates courteously acknowledged Sutter's title of Major General, bestowed upon him in 1853 along

with the honorary command of state troops known as the Sutter Rifles.

At Hock Farm Mrs. Bates saw her first cultivated rose since leaving New England. She further noted, "The house servants are all female. The General's carriage is drawn by two sleek-looking mules, and the driver's box is occupied by an Indian in fancy costume. Mrs. Sutter denies herself to all visitors."

The Sandwich Islanders who had traveled to California with Sutter were contract laborers, eight men and two women. One of the women, Manaiki, had been listed as Sutter's wife on the sea voyage. She bore him several children and was finally released to become the wife of Kanaka Harry, Sutter's devoted foreman.

Beginning in 1849 the first gold seekers established a network of towns in the foothills. Served by mule pack trains and later "prairie schooners" of wagons drawn by oxen, every home built along the way became a station, and some grew into towns. Hotels began as tent shelters and evolved into small log structures. As lumber mills opened, more elaborate facilities were built.

About 13 miles east of Marysville, a miner named Brown worked his way toward the hills. He stopped to cut the ripe wild hay at Brockman Ranch in May 1850 with a scythe he bought for $80 in gold dust, and set up a temporary camp. Right away Brown's scythe struck a rich vein of gold-studded quartz. He took out a fortune of $12,000 and quietly left the area later named for him, Brown's Valley.

Mills for crushing quartz surface ore operated there until John Rule, in 1852, erected a steam stamp mill. It served the deeper mine shafts that were sunk after the surface ore was depleted.

Twenty miles further into the foothills, the town of Dobbins started out as a ranch settled by William M. Dobbins and his brother Mark D. Dobbins in 1849. It soon became a mining town with the Dobbins Hotel situated at the end of the stage line. Nearby Indiana and Keystone creeks supported 400 to 500 miners in 1851 to 1852, on claims which measured 100 feet square and yielded an average of one ounce of gold per day.

Northeast of Dobbins, on the La Porte stage road, another Brown, Isaac E. Brown, built a sawmill in 1851. He sold the property in November 1852 to Martin Knox and P.E. Weeks, who operated the sawmill until 1857. When the town of Brownsville expanded, Knox and Weeks built a large hotel there in 1855, and in 1878 a young ladies' educational academy, the Knoxdale Institute, opened under the maternal supervision of Lena Knox, Martin's wife.

Challenge, which was located at a crossroads four miles above Brownsville

Above: This drawing portrays the Brownsville Hotel and the Knoxdale Institute, an educational academy for young ladies, as they appeared in 1879. The building that housed the institute still stands, transformed into Lucio's Restaurant, specializing in Southwestern cuisine. Courtesy, Yuba Feather Historical Association

A marching band parades past the Knox Hotel and Odd Fellows Hall at Brownsville in 1909. Courtesy, Yuba Feather Historical Association

and was central to many gold-bearing creeks, grew from a lumber mill which opened in 1856, owned by Union Lumber Company.

A.M. Leach bought the operation in 1874 and by 1879 had developed it from a single water-operated saw, cutting 18,000 board feet a day, into a boiler and steam engine mill producing 40,000 board feet daily. Between 1879 and 1883 some 135,000 board feet of Leach lumber went into the construction of a vee-

In 1899 students at the Challenge school were taught by Ida Ruff. A one-room facility held children of every age. Courtesy, Yuba Feather Historical Association

This early lumber-mill operated at Sharon Valley. The proprietor, L.T. Crane, lived close to his work; his residence is on the right. The location is at the junction of La Porte Road and Forbestown Road. Courtesy, Yuba Feather Historical Association

shaped flume. Over 30 miles long, the flume wound down the mountain to Moore's railroad station at Honcut Creek.

Crossing ravines over 100 feet deep required elaborate trestles and brave (or foolhardy) handlers with hooks to keep the flow steady. The flume carried wood products, shakes, lumber, and pine pitch for resin and turpentine, all at a rapid pace, with rushing, swift-plunging chutes at Challenge Hill and Hansonville Hill.

The cargo transported down the sometimes precipitous waterway was not exclusively lumber, however, as snow-packed "boat" boxes of trout and venison sped to homes, hotels, and restaurants in the valley. Nor was passage limited to commodities. Gamblers, dare-devils, and inebriates occasionally hitched on to the boats for a rapid ride, taunting fate or perhaps seeking a bleary "view of the elephant."

In 1884 the Leach Company's Challenge Mills extended the flume with a steam engine railroad from Challenge to Beanville. The mill complex expanded well into the 1880s to finally close down, insolvent, after the heavy snows of 1889.

Strawberry Valley, above the winter snow level at 3,500 feet, was first settled in 1848. Miners began to prospect the creeks and ravines by 1851. Rich diggings were struck along Deadwood Creek, at places called Kentucky Gulch, Rich Gulch, and Whiskey Gulch. The town grew to prominence as a resort area, popular for fishing, hunting, and

One of the Gold Rush towns, Strawberry Valley, survived to prosper into the 1900s. The North Star Hotel in Strawberry Valley was photographed by the McCurry Company, official photographers for the Sacramento Valley Exposition Commission, in 1915. Courtesy, Sacramento Valley Photo Survey and Yuba County Library

Leach County loggers patrolled the log flume with pickaroons to remove obstructions over the 30-mile course between Challenge and Moore's railroad station at Honcut. Courtesy, Yuba Feather Historical Association

Gold mining operations from simple panning to cradling, digging river diversion ditches, and building and operating flumes required lumber and partnerships as gold was found deeper underground. Courtesy, The Bancroft Library

camping, with a life-style well beyond that of those simply greedy for gold. Commercial and cultural services were established early: Wells Fargo stage, blacksmith, hotel, butcher, and carpenter shops. A public school opened in 1858, a Sunday school in 1860, and the Excelsior Literary and Library Association in 1867.

The easternmost settlement of Yuba County was Camptonville, which is located at an elevation of 2,850 feet and surrounded by rugged, timbered canyons. The town grew from a small hotel erected between the north and middle forks of the Yuba River in 1850 by the brothers J.M. and J. Campbell. Prospectors turned up in 1852, sank a shaft, and found rich stores of gold.

Camptonville grew to include stores, a Masonic Hall (still active), a dance hall, saloons, and a bowling alley. The popular blacksmith of the mountain community was Robert Campton. The town was named for him in 1854, the same year the wagon road was completed and the California Stage Company began making regular runs.

Below the junction of the three forks of the Yuba River at Rose Bar, where the Linda Company had once hoped to establish a head of navigation, John Rose and his partners George Kinlock and William J. Reynolds kept a store and raised cattle to feed the miners. It was at Rose Bar that Jonas Spect

had discovered the first Yuba County gold in June 1848. The original population of some 25 inhabitants had swollen to 2,000 miners by 1850.

Indians worked as laborers for a few years, content with payment in food and beads. They finally recognized the value of gold and upped their demands to modest cash wages.

Large numbers of immigrants from the oppressed and overpopulated Canton province of China also provided cheap labor. Treated almost as slaves, the Chinese held onto their first wages in gold dust. As white miners moved from depleted diggings on to new claims, the Chinese bought the discarded territories and worked them steadily to substantial profit.

Small partnerships and then larger companies formed as the gold extraction process grew more complex and required new skills, cooperation, lumber, and above all, water.

Water was essential to every process of prospecting, from simple panning by one individual to cradling— whereby four men worked together shoveling, washing, rocking, and straining—through sluicing. Altering the courses of streams and rivers in the interests of mining became a common practice.

In 1854 hydraulic mining developed upriver from Rose Bar. The most elaborate and profitable method of gold extraction yet to be devised, hydraulic mining transfigured the land, hills, towns, streams, rivers, and valley to a massive degree.

Hydraulic mining operated by directing a powerful stream of water at a hillside and washing away the land to reveal the gold. The by-product was debris, enough to raise the Yuba riverbed above the level of the town of Marysville and destroy rich farmland in the valley.

Debris from hydraulic mining companies at Timbuctoo and Smartsville buried Rose Bar. Rose Bar, Saw-Mill Bar, Lander's Bar, Kennebec Bar, Sand Hill, and Cape Horn, all mining camps along the Yuba River, disappeared under as much as 200 feet of debris.

Fortunes won from gold mining, by whatever means, led to the founding of dynasties and towns, enhanced or destroyed families, and made fools of many. Three small banks in the Yuba-Sutter region shipped to the East $10 million in gold dust in 1857 alone.

Fortunes of gold also traveled in bags strapped underneath clothing. One

Hydraulic mining, shown here, eroded hillsides and filled rivers with debris. There were no controls on the practice until the Sawyer Decision of 1884 declared the dumping of debris into rivers illegal. Courtesy, Yuba Feather Historical Association

miner prospected the foothills for many bitter months. He wrote piteous letters to his wife in Indiana, inquiring after her health and that of their numerous children. He once enclosed a dollar in gold dust.

Finally our hero made a substantial strike and booked passage on a ship, planning to return in grand style after his indecorous departure on foot. He strapped the gold to his belt and boarded. The ship ran aground off Cape Horn,

In 1862 hydraulic mining drastically eroded this hillside in Timbuctoo. The foundations of the town filled the rivers and emptied into San Francisco Bay. Courtesy, Yuba Feather Historical Association

and the man was thrown overboard. He cut the heavy fortune off his body barely in time to save himself from drowning.

Rescued, yet in poor condition, he was transported up the Mississippi River from New Orleans and arrived home in Indiana only to die within the week. His wife lived to the age of 90 and never re-married. His great-grandson inherited the knife which sent the gold to the bottom of the sea and reveres his pioneer heritage to this day.

By 1853 quick strikes had ended, and 2,000 miners headed off to new dis-coveries along the Fraser River. Again in 1860, the year Abraham Lincoln was elected president, news of a major strike in Washoe County, Nevada, drew away another 2,000 transients.

Nevertheless, by the mid-1860s a population stabilized at around 11,000 in Yuba County and 6,000 in Sutter County.

With the decline in Gold Rush traf-fic, farmers and ranchers returned to prominence in the valley and foothills. The first crop planted in the area had been Cordua's small field of wheat in 1845. Soon after, Theodore Sicard

Chinese laborers, shown here working at the winepresses, excelled in agricultural efforts; however, white job seekers began to resent the competition from the Chinese, who worked cheaply. Courtesy, The Bancroft Library

planted 15 acres yielding 60 bushels each. Sutter harvested the wild grains with 200 Indians and sickles and knives.

Wheat, however, was still mainly imported from Chile, Australia, and Virginia. Not until 1856 did local farmers become aware of the potential for abundant, high quality local wheat. Production increased enough to meet the needs of local consumers and then came to a standstill.

In 1861 a few citizens, derided as lunatics, overrode local protest and shipped a cargo of wheat to Liverpool.

The grain reached England in excellent condition. A second successful shipment astonished the provincials and conquered skepticism. Whereas Virginia wheat required large temperature-controlled drying rooms, the sun and hot, dry summer air of Sutter County quickly ripened kernels spread on pans after being harvested.

Suddenly agriculture replaced gold fever, stirred new excitement and inventiveness, and paved a more reliable road to prosperity.

California's first agricultural fair took

The steamer *Red Bluff* is seen here passing Meridian Bridge on its regular trip between Red Bluff and Sacramento, circa 1912. Courtesy, Special Collections, Meriam Library, California State University, Chico, and Sutter County Community Memorial Museum

Moon's Ferry, which crossed the Sacramento River to Colusa, west of the Buttes, was licensed in 1867. Fifty cents carried a horse and carriage over the water, until tollbridges were installed to serve the increasing traffic. Courtesy, Mary Aaron Museum

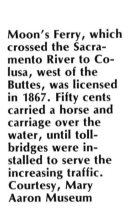

place in Marysville in 1853. A large pavilion was built in 1858 for the California State Fair and for future fairs and exhibitions at Cortez Square.

Vineyards, orchards, and gardens were established at Hock Farm and at Claude Chana's place along the Bear River. A serious farmer, Chana had brought ploughs with him in 1846. A threshing machine was developed in 1851 and an iron harrow in 1852.

Drainage projects in Sutter County opened the tule lands to farming and destroyed much of the waterfowl habitat. The 17,000 acres under cultivation in 1858 were to increase over the next 100 years to 360,000, in a county with a total of 395,000 acres.

The first gristmill was established at Chana's place. Barley, corn, and hay became the dominant crops. Soon grapes were developed for wine, and orchards began fruiting. Large canneries followed and developed into a major industry.

Lumber early became a valuable commodity. Along the rivers and banks grew luxuriant stands of oak and sycamore, said to be so thick a man could ride from the Yuba River to the Bear River in their shade. These hardwoods fell to fuel steamers and stoves. Pine, cedar, and fir flumed down the mountain for construction projects as well as for export.

On a single day early in August 1851, seven steamers full of freight arrived at the Marysville wharf. Yuba City's frequent attempts to garner commercial trade failed, however, because of awkward bridge transport.

Beginning in 1843 when Sutter hired Nicolaus Altgeier to operate a ferry across the Feather River between Nicolaus and Hock Farm, more rivers became accessible. A ferry license was granted by the Court of Sessions for a Marysville-Yuba City crossing in 1850, and another was granted the same year for the Sacramento at Vernon.

Toll bridges followed, although most fell quickly because of floods or the weight of ox teams. Nevertheless, in 1854 John C. Fall became proprietor of the Feather River span and built a sturdy structure. Unfortunately, this bridge succumbed in the winter of 1860 to 1861, when water and mining debris inundated the entire valley.

Beginning with canoes and whalers, the Feather River served as a major trading artery. Large schooners sailed up the Feather River as far as Nicolaus in 1849. Nicolaus Altgeier of that settlement brought supplies regularly from Sacramento aboard his 15-ton launch powered by wind and oars.

After hydraulic mining filled the rivers with debris, steam navigation to Marysville became impossible during the

dry season. A small warehouse was then erected in Yuba City to receive goods. Before railroads took over the bulk of transport, low-water vessels and barges plied the rivers, loaded with grain and produce for the downstream trip, and manufactured items for the trip upriver from San Francisco and Sacramento.

Surveys and negotiations for railroads had taken place since 1851. The California Northern Railroad started between Oroville and Marysville in 1864; in 1868 the California and Oregon Railroad was granted right-of-way by the Common Council of Marysville. The California and Oregon Railroad then laid track from Sacramento through Linda into Marysville in 1869. The road crossed the Feather River north of Yuba City and helped the town of Live Oak develop into a thriving farm center.

For the 1875 state fair at Cortez Square in Marysville, Sutter County introduced a triumphal array of local crops: cling peaches, walnuts, a special wheat, and the new Thompson seedless grape, which had been discovered in 1870.

Schools opened as the first batch of

The Levi Strauss Company, aided by Hamilton Brown, shoemaker, outfitted miners and farmers at Nicolaus in 1898. Courtesy, Special Collections, Meriam Library, California State University, Chico, and Sutter County Community Memorial Museum

Incorporated in 1874, Wheatland was located at Johnson's Crossing on the Bear River. The livery stable, shown in a 1912 photo, was one of 40 businesses established by 1879. Courtesy, Miriam Griffiths and Meriam Library, California State University, Chico

In 1885, at the confluence of the Yuba and Feather rivers, Marysville was becoming established and Yuba City was developing farming. Courtesy, The Bancroft Library

pioneer progeny reached the appropriate age. Linda School, located on the trail between Marysville and Johnson's Crossing, started classes in 1855 with 36 pupils. Six years later another 350 students matriculated.

By 1880 the local student population had increased to 2,487, of whom 78 were classified as "indian and negro." The sizable but disregarded Chinese community taught its children at home in the Chinese and English languages. In the hills and outlying areas, 47 one-room schoolhouses sprang up to serve an additional 2,123 rural students.

Little agricultural wealth would endure in Yuba County once hydraulic mining began. The rich bottomland along the rivers was cultivated only until 1860. During that year of massive flooding, the clogged Yuba River, heavy and black with sediment, spread over the banks and across the valley to devastate most of Yuba County's fertile land.

All of the bottomland along the Yuba and Bear rivers was destroyed by 1879. Five to 10 feet of mining debris extended as much as a mile and a half back from the banks and spared only the southern portion of Claude Chana's rich lands, now Wheatland. The profits from nature's abundant gifts passed back to Sutter County.

The small but prospering farm community of Wheatland provided music instruction for high school students, who formed this orchestra in 1914. Photo by Henry M. Seron. Courtesy, Special Collections, Meriam Library, California State University, Chico

CHAPTER
IV

CONDUCTORS
AND
INSTRUMENTS

Theodor Cordua. The foundation of Marysville was laid by a man of probable Spanish ancestry, Theodor Cordua, whose family had settled in the north of Germany during the sixteenth or seventeenth century. This adventurous merchant leased Sutter's northern 11 leagues on the east bank of the Feather River and added to it the land north to Honcut Creek and west to the foothills. Cordua named his property New Mecklenburg in hopes (unsuccessful, as it turned out) of attracting settlers from his home in Germany.

Unlike the authoritarian Sutter, Cordua treated his 6,000 to 7,000 Indian residents as employees rather than as subjects. Both men paid wages and board, though Sutter kept his Indian soldiers confined in stables without water or toilet facilities, while Cordua's workers were allowed to remain in tribal villages.

Cordua's memoirs record his first agricultural efforts in California:

In the beginning I had to struggle with unspeakable difficulties. The virgin soil

The Wednesday Embroidery Club met at Meridian Hotel, under the proprietorship of Mrs. Boyd Taylor, in 1912. Courtesy, Special Collections, Meriam Library, California State University, Chico

Theodor Cordua's manners, education, and business expertise influenced the life-style of the first settlers at the confluence of the Yuba and Feather rivers. He protected the civil rights of his employees and dispensed justice with honesty and fairness. This is an artist's conception of Cordua as he appeared in 1842 when he was the first white settler in the region. Drawing by David Giles

had to be broken with the plowshare, and it was extremely difficult to instruct the laborers on account of the language. The first good ox-hide served as a mattress, and the saddle as a pillow, the stumps of trees as a table and chairs . . .

Under such circumstances, and especially since I saw everything around me in a wild state, my courage changed sometimes to despondency and all my dreams in anticipation of a pleasant life in this beautiful wilderness seemed to fade. But with persistent industry and courageous efforts I finally reached my goal, and—since a human being is a victim of habit—I became satisfied with everything that had been foreign to me at first.

In the spring of 1843, I was in the happy position to erect structures of clay, frame, and straw, and to build several enclosures for the cattle and horses on my ranch. I could lay out gardens and fields and provide them with fences and ditches.

Cattle, it may be noted, were initially used by whites for tallow and hides, the carcasses given to Indians for food.

Cordua served as messenger in the Mexican campaign of Governor Manuel Micheltorena, who enlisted several hundred freed convicts to defend California in 1845. The campaign in which Sutter and Cordua served as "unnecessary associates" ended in defeat, although with Cordua honorably commissioned and Sutter suffering disgrace.

As a well-established settler when the Gold Rush began, Cordua was obliged to extend hospitality freely to all newcomers and to remain at home to protect his holdings. He also was obliged to take a partner and unfortunately selected Charles Covillaud.

I soon learned that he was a very bad fellow without any character. He acted entirely against my interest and did not pay any attention to our contract. Since

there were hardly any laws, the one who owned the most had to suffer. This and other things induced me to sell the other half of my property to Covillaud's brothers-in-law, Mr. Nye and Mr. Forster [sic] for twenty thousand dollars.

Indeed, Martin Nye had been Cordua's majordomo for several years and was known as a cattle thief, while Mr. William M. Foster was "every inch a gentleman."

Cordua meanwhile wandered through Northern California, unable to recoup his losses, and "took to the bottle."

My health was ruined, my future prospects very hazy, and the memory of the past few years so painful that I disliked to stay here any longer. In the ten years which I had spent in California I had not spent one hundred dollars for clothing and pleasure, and yet hundreds of thousands of dollars had disappeared . . . One misfortune after another had come— fire, water, swindle, and theft—until the devil had taken everything.

Before returning to Germany, Cordua took a final trip in 1852 to his former New Mecklenburg. There he found one of the most densely populated districts in the Sacramento Valley, Marysville, with about 20,000 white residents. The Indian villages had disappeared from the river banks; hotels, churches, and theaters covered his ranch; and his gardens lay occupied by several hundred warehouses. The river itself now carried 15 to 20 steamers, its once crystalline water muddy with gold washings.

John Sutter's Waning Days. Living quietly at Hock Farm, Sutter continued his horticultural and agricultural studies while his property was gradually lost to squatters, bandits, and natural disasters.

Massive flooding and mining debris in 1861 to 1862 covered all but a corner of Hock Farm and destroyed the orchards. Finally, early in the morning of June 21, 1866, a fire broke out, probably the work of an arsonist.

The Marysville *Appeal* reported that Sutter's dwelling was "completely destroyed—home, clothing, pictures, busts, curiosities that had been accumulating for the last forty years, except a few medals and his family portraits . . . There is no insurance."

Sutter and his family moved to the Moravian region of Pennsylvania and built a home at Lititz with a small government annuity, granted through the efforts of the Associated Pioneers of the Territorial Days of California. Sutter's last years were spent in frequent visits to Washington, D.C., where he hoped to regain title or compensation for his land.

In 1876 California historian Hubert H. Bancroft traveled to Lititz to record Sutter's reminiscences. Bancroft noted that of his betrayal by a trusted friend, Sutter commented, "I should have sent my Indians." Bancroft observed, "It seems that the gentle Swiss always found his beloved aboriginals far less treacherous than the whiteskinned parasites."

Sam Brannan, founder of Yuba City, adventurer, Mormon elder, capitalist, publisher, vigilante—and many other things—took over Sacramento when Fort Sutter collapsed in 1849. He successfully drove a wedge between John Sutter and his son by prompting the son to remove the town to the embarcadero, originally a mere landing for Sutter's Fort.

Born in Maine, Brannan had learned the printing trade as an apprentice and failed a few times in the business. He had turned up in New York as an elder of the Latter-day Saints and was in charge of some 300 Mormon men, women, and children seeking the promised land.

While Brigham Young led a pilgrimage west by land, Brannan's wealthier

Hock Farm was destroyed by fire in 1866, and the Sutter family moved to Pennsylvania. The farm was later rebuilt by Christian Schmidt, as seen here in 1879, and much of its productivity was restored. Courtesy, Mary Aaron Museum

group traveled by ship, from New York to Yerba Buena.

Aboard the *Brooklyn* Brannan carried a printing press, two complete flour mills, and other necessities. The arrival of the Mormons at Yerba Buena on August 3, 1846, suddenly populated that outpost with 50 or 60 souls, two of them women.

Upon arrival Brannan was accused by a woman in his flock of misappropriating funds. He began a newspaper, the *California Star*, bought property on Yerba Buena Plaza, and engaged in extensive building projects. He eventually owned one-fifth of San Francisco, one-fourth of Sacramento, and all of Yuba City, which was located on 640 acres purchased from Sutter in 1849.

The first successful exploiter of the wild and golden west, Brannan spent no time actually mining gold. Instead he provided builders, funds, and materials for Sutter's mills. Then, as gold fever spread and lesser saints began mining in earnest, Brannan used his position to levy a 10 percent tithe against their findings. One suspicious miner inquired whether Brannan was in fact entitled to this share. "Sure he is," a deputy told him, "as long as you're fool enough to pay it."

These tithes meanwhile were requested by Brigham Young at Salt Lake, but Brannan agreed to release them only upon a receipt from the Lord Himself. The upshot was excommunication for the richest man in California at that time.

Brannan was above all an innovator. One example was his formation of the Vigilance Committee in San Francisco in 1851. The forces he organized ended a series of arsonous fires which had six times leveled San Francisco; but as the fires ended and the level of criminality approached his own, Brannan moved on to other adventures.

Like the affable Sutter, Brannan increasingly functioned while "under the

influence." His intemperance soon drove his wife and four children to residence in Germany; to his moral credit, however, they were supplied with abundant funds.

In 1859 Brannan left San Francisco and Sacramento for the Napa Valley, where he sought to exploit the hot springs at Calistoga. Only the distillery survived. Brannan lost his shirt, drank the dregs of his fortune, and headed downhill.

Destitute and derelict, he settled in San Diego with a Mexican woman for his final years of dissipation. Then suddenly the Mexican government elected to begin reparations for a long-forgotten mutual enterprise and sent him $49,000.

The old man, nearly 70, quit drinking, recovered his health, and spent the entire sum of $49,000 repaying his debts. He died in San Diego on May 14, 1889, lacking the funds for his own burial.

Augustus Le Plongeon. Marysville is indebted to another controversial figure, Augustus Le Plongeon, who designed the town in 1850. The broad streets and abundant trees and parks, which residents and visitors from forty-niners to present-day tourists have found attractive, reflect Le Plongeon's vision. His design retained the natural beauty of the

Right: Augustus Le Plongeon, an educated aristocrat, was responsible for the original plan for Marysville, which included numerous parks and spacious streets. Courtesy, Yuba County Library

Le Plongeon returned to South America after his significant role in the planning of Marysville and Linda. There Le Plongeon researched the connection between the Mayan and Egyptian cultures. Courtesy, Yuba County Library

graceful river landscape.

Le Plongeon was born to all the prominence, romance, and advantages of the landed gentry to which John Sutter spent his life aspiring. A nephew of its feudal lord, Le Plongeon was born on the island of Jersey, a British colony off the coast of France.

Both French and English were spoken in his home. He attended a military academy at Caen, France, as well as the Polytechnic Institute of Paris. His well-rounded education included the humanities along with science and technology.

In 1846 Le Plongeon and a fellow student bought a small boat. Bound for the Pacific Ocean and with Le Plongeon as navigator, they headed across the Atlantic Ocean and around Cape Horn. A storm wrecked the boat and only one seaman and Le Plongeon survived. Ending up in Valparaiso, Chile, Le Plongeon began teaching college students there. He was well placed then for travel to California the moment news of the gold discovery broke.

He arrived at the confluence of the Yuba and Feather rivers to make the acquaintance of the two French land developers, Covillaud and Sicard. Le Plongeon, with his facility for language and his sur-

veying skills, easily ingratiated himself with the city planners. As payment for designing the town, he received five lots along the Plaza on E Street, which were valued at $1,150. By his departure in 1854, the property yielded $30,000.

Le Plongeon's later activities as an archaeologist studying the possibility of communication between the ancient Egyptian and Mayan cultures were highly controversial. He was married late in life to a young musician and mystic, Alice Dixon. The couple took up the cause of a French missionary and archaeologist, Abbe Brasseur; inspired by his writings they promoted Plato's legend of Atlantis in an attempt to establish cultural and linguistic links between Europe and America by positing a single land mass, Atlantis, which had comprised both continents.

Professional archaeological societies, however, dismissed any serious discussion of the legend as history. Finally, amid public accusations that he was confusing spirituality with science, Le Plongeon was denied permission to read his papers at professional meetings. Today his work is credited by geophysicists as well as by Rosicrucians, Theosophists, and groups that embrace the Atlantis theory.

Mary Murphy Covillaud, 1830-1867, gave birth to five children in her namesake town, Marysville. Her short, productive life was devoted to the care of others, including Donner party orphans, of which she was one. Courtesy, Yuba County Library

Mary Murphy Covillaud. The typical wilderness family in 1847, a white man with an Indian squaw and unacknowledged offspring, began to alter with the arrival of Mary Murphy. A teenage survivor of the Donner party, Mary had been left in a snowbound cabin to care for five small children and her ailing mother after the first rescue team had arrived and departed. She writes in her diary:

Men from Fort Sutter reached those of us who were still alive. We were a miserable lot, sustained mostly by a will to live, and by prayer. On February 19, I was taken out with my brother and twenty-three others. Left behind was my blind mother and my baby brother, Simon.

We made the tortuous journey through the snow before we came to the headwaters of the Yuba river where there were mules to carry us down to Johnson's ranch. My mother later passed away in her cabin amid the corpses of others who had already gone to their eternal rest.

I stayed several days at the ranch, enjoying the comforts of civilization again, but I never could erase from my mind the sight of the dying people left behind at the lake.

Knowing I was uncertain of my future, and having fallen in love with me, Mr. Johnson proposed marriage. In June 1847, at the age of eighteen I became Mrs. Johnson. For several months I was busy serving to all of Mr. Johnson's wishes, doing his cooking and washing and trying to make a home out of a cattle ranch.

I knew he was a crude man and sometimes I overlooked his faults, but I could not love a man who abused me with the rest of the ranch hands.

He proved to be a drunken sot. Because of that I got in touch with the rest of my family and secured an annulment of my marriage from the church.

My married sister, Sarah, and her husband, Mr. Foster, was working at the Cordua ranch with my older brother William. The superintendant of the ranch was Charles Covillaud who had come west and crossed the mountains a few weeks before we did. It wasn't long before I was introduced to Charles, and from that moment on, I knew I had fallen in love with a gentleman. Charles and I were married on Christmas day at Sutter's Fort.

Charles soon bought the Cordua ranch and became a successful merchant, providing the miners who were on their way to the diggins in 'forty nine with food and supplies.

The election of Stephen J. Field as alcalde of the settlement at the confluence of the Yuba and Feather rivers took place on January 18, 1850. That same evening Captain Edward Power from St. Louis proposed the name of Marysville for the settlement. In this way he wished to honor Mary Murphy Covillaud as a paragon of graciousness where previously harsh realities had prevailed.

Mary Covillaud continued to serve her community, nursing the sick and assisting others in distress for 17 more years until she died in 1867.

Stephen J. Field was an attorney of fearless initiative who introduced law and order to the rollicking, boisterous, gold rush town of Marysville. Eventually Field ended up on the bench of the U.S. Supreme Court. From Field, *Early Days in California,* 1968. Courtesy, Yuba County Library

Stephen J. Field. In 1850 as the first alcalde of Marysville under Mexican law, Stephen J. Field inaugurated the town's first judicial system and helped form the California legislature. A man of considerable integrity and courage, Field survived financial difficulties brought on by the antagonism of District Court Judge Turner and eventually returned to practicing law.

He furthered Mary Covillaud's efforts to bring refinement to the town of Marysville and was responsible for drawing up its city charter. In 1857 Field participated in the first California legislature. He left Marysville that year to serve on the Supreme Court of California, where he later became chief justice.

When he was appointed by President Abraham Lincoln to the Supreme Court of the United States in 1863, Field was confirmed without opposition. Field's colleague, Judge Joseph G. Baldwin, had this to say as Field departed California for Washington, D.C.:

Like most men who have risen to distinction in the United States, Judge Field commenced his career without the advantages of wealth, and he prosecuted it without the factitious aids of family influence or patronage . . .

He brought to the practice of his profession a mind stored with professional learning, and embellished with rare scholarly attainments. He was distinguished at the bar for his fidelity to his clients, for untiring industry, great care and accuracy in the preparation of his cases, uncommon legal acumen, and extraordinary solidity of judgment.

The land titles of the State have received from his hand their permanent protection, and this alone should entitle him to the lasting gratitude of the bar and the people.

Above: An exceptional example of early Gothic Revival architecture, the Mary Aaron Museum was founded by Frank Aaron to honor his mother. Photo by Henry Sackrider. Courtesy, California State Library

Facing page: These venerable trees in Cortez Square, shown here circa 1915, contributed to the city's character, but progress eventually eliminated these living monuments from the center of town. Photo by Henry Sackrider. Courtesy, Yuba County Library

Mrs. D.B. Bates sailed from Baltimore in July 1850 aboard a ship, the *Nonantum* of Boston, of which her husband was master. The *Nonantum* carried 1,050 tons of wet but combustible coal in the hold. The combustibility became noticeable some 800 miles from the Falkland Islands.

After experiencing three fires at sea and catching rides on subsequent ships, the Bateses arrived in Marysville in 1851. Mrs. Bates wrote extensively in her journal, which was published in 1857. It richly detailed her travels and the character of the town and its personalities:

I was perfectly delighted with the appearance of this little inland city. Every little collection of canvas stores and dwellings in California were denominated cities. Marysville, at that time boasted of several large frame buildings, among which were the hotels. It was ranked the third city in regard to size and improvements in Upper California.

Ladies were very scarce in Marysville; at this time there were not more than half a dozen, at the most, who were deserving of the appellation. Comparatively speaking, there were no children . . .

There were assembled representatives from every clime and country on the face of the globe. The European, the Asiatic, the African, the Anglo-Saxon, the Sandwich-Islander, all, whose general interests and pursuits were so varied, had here convened for one and the same purpose—to get gold. No law was acknowledged except Lynch law; and the penalty for offenses, so summarily enforced by the vigilance committees, served admirably to keep in check the murderous, villainous propensities of too

many of the refugees from justice from all parts of the world.

Mrs. Bates took over supervision of the domestics department of the new Tremont Hotel while her husband searched for a suitable occupation. He found it as a hotel proprietor, and eventually they managed the Atlantic Hotel together until Mrs. Bates collapsed with fatigue and a fever which lasted three months.

Rescued from the prolonged fever

by her brother, who came from the East, and by a ministering angel of Mary Covillaud's persuasion, Mrs. Bates departed in 1854 for her cherished home in Massachusetts—alone.

Although no reason for her solo flight appears, Mrs. Bates' detailed references to the evils of drink and gambling in her journal suggest a familiarity with these subjects which she may have hoped to leave behind with Mr. Bates.

Generally, the women of the fron-

A modern dredger continues to operate in the Yuba gold fields, but today the fields serve another purpose: they provide an ideal flight path for Beale Air Force Base. Photo by David Giles

tier did not engage in political activities, although they had a profound moral and religious influence on the towns they inhabited. A few, like Mrs. D.B. Bates, recorded their observations of society.

General Edward Fitzgerald Beale

was born to a family of naval heroes and followed in their steps to attend the naval academy. He arrived in California in 1846 and distinguished himself with Kit Carson during the war with Mexico. He became a trusted courier of the United States government and made frequent transcontinental journeys from 1846 on. Beale in fact brought reports of the Mexican defeat to Washington. Soon thereafter he carried the first gold nugget from California, which would infect Eastern adventurers with gold fever.

Then, as the fever subsided, Beale rescued Commodore Robert Stockton's failing mining and real estate business by transforming the available resources into a statewide transportation system.

In 1852, with friction increasing between the Indians and the white settlers, President Millard Fillmore averted calamity by appointing Beale Commissioner of Indian Affairs. Beale held the commission for five years and developed the celebrated Camel Corps, which was made up of pack animals suited to desert travel across the southern United States.

Trusted by the United States government and the Indians alike, Beale worked tirelessly to resolve conflicts before they erupted, not only in the West but also in areas directly affected by the Civil War. He finally retired to a 200,000-acre ranch at Tejon on the Tehachapi Ridge within an area controlled by bandits, most of whom had resorted to crime after abuse by white settlers. Beale alone among whites was safe among them, respected for his honesty and fairness.

Camp Beale came into being in 1942 at the site of the old army post at Camp Far West. A training base for the 13th Armored Division and the 81st and 96th Infantry Divisions, Camp Beale also held prisoners of war during World War II.

The United States Air Force took over the facility in 1948 and located units of the Strategic Air Command there in 1959. Now assigned to Camp Beale, the Ninth Strategic Reconnaissance Wing flies KC-135, U-2, and SR-71 planes.

CHAPTER
V

DISSONANCE

Floods strike at the hearts of Yuba and Sutter counties at about 20-year intervals. Massive floodings occur every 100 years or so and ravage orchards, homes, and sometimes lives. Nevertheless, despite the valley's hot, dry, and rainless summers, it is rarely threatened by drought.

Dams, levees, and canals control some of nature's caprices; hydraulic mining, pesticide pollution, and clear-cutting timber threaten to offset the benefit of these controls. Indeed, the wilderness inhabited by Indians a mere 200 years ago is now suffering disfigurement.

Indians recalled major floods in the Sacramento Valley in 1805 and again in 1825 to 1826. Gold seekers experienced prolonged rains, heavy snows, mud, and plummeting streams during the winter of 1849 to 1850. Many starved to death in the high country at that time.

Then came the winter of 1861 to 1862, when rainfall measured between 115 and 179 inches. Flooding inundated the valley with silt and mining debris that buried homes and destroyed or-

Artist Charles Nahl dramatized conflicts between man and nature, as in this drawing of a flood, circa 1878. From Pennoyer, *This Was California,* 1938. Courtesy, Special Collections, Meriam Library, California State University, Chico

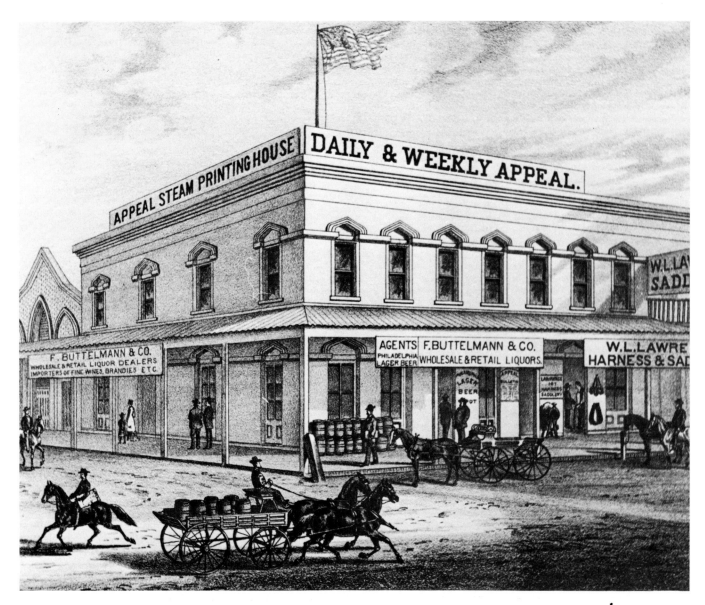

The *Daily Appeal* was first published in January 1860 as a politically independent newspaper. Six months later, B.P. Avery changed the editorial emphasis to Republican. The newspaper deviated from this only once, when it supported John Bidwell, the Independent candidate for governor, in 1875. The *Appeal* merged with the *Daily National Democrat* in 1861. Courtesy, Maybelle Arnold

chards along the Yuba River. The entire valley—cities, homesteads, and fields—filled with water. The *Alta California* reported deaths on January 23, 1862:

This record must embrace white men alone, for Chinese have been lost by the hundreds. On the Yuba alone, there were fifty deaths; in Placer County, one hundred fifty; according to the Courier . . . *Chinamen say the number of their countrymen destroyed in the State by the December floods alone was about 500.*

The fresh water draining into San Francisco Bay that year was sufficient to cover the bay surface 18 to 24 inches deep. Fishermen caught freshwater varieties there for two to three months; water was brackish in the Farallone Islands.

Meanwhile hydraulic mining increased until the next major flood in 1875. The Yuba flatlands lay under 25 to 30 feet of silt, which destroyed rich bottomland, crops, and farms. Conflict soon erupted between the farmers and the miners.

After numerous face-to-face confrontations, the flat-landers went to the courts. *People v. Gold Run Mining Co.* was decided in favor of the valley inhabitants in 1881, although hydraulic mining continued unimpeded.

In a pivotal U.S. Circuit Court decision, Judge Lorenzo Sawyer in 1884 rendered hydraulic mining legal, but dumping debris into state waters illegal. In response miners built cosmetic structures and added armed guards to their operations. Meanwhile farmers formed the Anti-Debris Association to implement the new law; however, its representatives were vulnerable to bribery by mining officials.

Editor Milton McWhorter of the Marysville *Daily Democrat* entered the fray in 1886. He declared that U.S. Marshal T.G. Robinson, in charge of injunctions against bootleg mining,

can sit day after day on the banks of a hydraulic claim while the pipes play in full view, yet cannot see their piping. If the good citizens of the valley feel safe with the valley interests in the hands of a man that "a little blaze" can drive from a house of ill fame in his shirt tail when he should be guarding their homes from the effects of the monitors, they are more trusting than we are.

Burly Marshal Robinson reacted by publicly threatening McWhorter's life. The slightly built, 118-pound McWhorter armed himself with a Smith and Wesson 44. A noisy skirmish took place outside the state legislature and ended with Robinson dead. The case of *People v. McWhorter* charged the latter with manslaughter.

McWhorter, out on bail, continued to print invectives against the hydraulic miners, who rallied to support the prosecution in the case. Farmers backed McWhorter. Gamblers offered two-to-one odds for conviction. Attorney Grove Johnson, father of California's innovative governor Hiram Johnson, argued for the defense and gained an acquittal.

Miners fought back with their own legislation, the Caminetti Act. Adopted in 1893, it placed hydraulic mining under the supervision of the California Debris Commission. The Commission, however, mandated debris dams which the miners discovered to be cost prohibitive— along, then, with hydraulic mining.

In 1888 William T. Ellis, Jr., entered politics as county supervisor in Marysville at the age of 22. Later he was elected

Dredgers replaced hydraulic mining after legislation prevented the dumping of debris into rivers. Courtesy, Yuba Feather Historical Association

mayor, served two terms, and was a partner in his father's successful merchandising business.

Ellis became president of the Levee Commission in 1900 and devoted his life, including seven years' service on the State Reclamation Board, to flood control.

His efforts built the present system of levees and established river gauges and emergency telephone service during rainy seasons. Data collected by Ellis over many years now make it possible to predict water levels and expected times of crest in the valley. Otherwise the fast-moving Yuba permits only a brief warning period as rising waters plunge down the Sierra Nevada.

In Ellis' opinion, the reclamation of the flood plains, which had made storage basins into farmland, had deleterious effects. He cited the loss of 364,695 acres of storage basin, writing in 1939:

Before all this reclamation occurred, the flood waters "hesitated" at these various basins and filled each "with a good big drink," then continued onward to discharge into the bays, thence to the sea.

Now the flood waters no longer have these basins at which to hesitate, they travel by fast express . . . flood waters have not the opportunity to seep down in the ground and, in my opinion, this has been a large contributing factor in the rather alarming lowering of the water table, necessitating deeper and deeper wells for irrigation purposes.

One reclamation project Ellis particularly questioned was the Fremont Weir, 9,200 feet of solid concrete blocking Sutter Bypass floodwaters from the Yolo Basin to a level three and a half feet above the Bypass floor.

The magnitude of the discharge of the Sacramento River and its tributaries, when compared with other major rivers,

In order to harness the rivers, the Yuba Electric Power Company engaged 200 workers to construct the Colgate powerhouse on the north fork of the Yuba River near Dobbins. High voltage transmission to Sacramento began on September 5, 1899, and led to advances in hydroelectric power. Courtesy, Special Collections, Meriam Library, California State University, Chico

indicates a higher rate of flow from a far smaller drainage area. For example, the Missouri River has a drainage area of 527,000 square miles with a recorded discharge of 546,000 acre-feet per second at its mouth; in 1907 the Sacramento discharged 600,000 acre-feet per second from a 26,000-square-mile area.

At the time John Sutter arrived, the placid, slow-moving waters of the lower Sacramento River offered lush breeding ponds for marauding hordes of carnivorous mosquitoes. Swarms of zinging, stinging welt-raisers plagued settlers through the hot summers, morning and evening. The only defense was to swat each attacker after it was already heavy with its victim's blood and thus slow to

escape.

Other adversities plagued the region. San Francisco was gutted by a rash of six great fires which, having begun on Christmas Eve, 1849, and continued through June 1851, led to the state's first organized resistance to crime, Sam Brannan's Vigilance Committee of volunteers. Until it was founded only criminals were well organized.

A regiment of New York soldiers under the command of Colonel Jonathan D. Stevenson had arrived in San Francisco in 1847 to complete the conquest of California and ensure its peaceful settlement. The members of Stevenson's Regiment, drifters and former Tammany Hall devotees, remained in California after the regiment itself disbanded.

These militaristic cast-offs reorganized secretly under Lieutenant Sam Roberts. They took the official title of "The Supreme Order of the Star-Spangled Banner," parent of the area's present-day Ku Klux Klan. These "patriots" were opposed to Roman Catholics and "greasers," and their avowed purpose was to keep America "pure."

With Mexico's laws rendered inoperative and no California law firmly in place, these ruffians burned and plundered without hindrance. Known to citizens as the "Hounds," they paraded, armed, in motley uniforms; in fact they took over the city.

The Vigilance Committee eventually wrested control of San Francisco from the "Hounds" with due process of law. However, as the city lacked a jail or the funds for deportation, the criminals were banished to inner cities such as Sacramento and Marysville. Yet, as lawlessness and bigotry among the gold seekers increased, the "Hounds" easily

This postcard photo depicts Pennington on the north edge of Sutter County after it was devastated by fire in 1914. The town did not rebuild. Courtesy, Special Collections, Meriam Library, California State University, Chico, and Sutter County Memorial Museum

In 1920 most area firefighters were volunteers, including these men gathered in front of the Marysville firehouse. The station pet is apparently fascinated by the program being broadcast by the radio, still quite a novelty at the time. Courtesy, Sacramento History Center

found compatriots in their new territory.

Fires of unknown origin erupted. One, which broke out during Stephen J. Field's lawmaking reforms, was set in order to cover the traces of a murder. The Sutter County Courthouse itself was gutted by a fire in 1899. Yuba City was stricken in 1907, Pennington in 1914.

Fires grew so frequent as to finally prompt Marysville residents in 1879 to erect brick buildings in the downtown area.

While San Francisco was deporting its criminals to the inland cities, oppression and overcrowding worldwide drove a vast array of ethnic groups to Yuba and Sutter counties.

Chinese from Canton province had arrived early in California, working the gold fields and laying transcontinental railroad tracks over the Sierra Nevada. They established a sizable community in Marysville, and in 1861 four farms at the edge of town were deeded to Chinese owners. By 1882 so much wealth had accrued to these diligent, steady workers that Marysville's Chinatown had become a religious and cultural center, with 48 Chinese-owned businesses.

Because throughout California white laborers demanded higher pay, growers continued to hire Chinese workers at

premacy. As late as 1913 the California Land Act prohibited Japanese ownership of agricultural lands.

Violence has preyed on the region of Yuba and Sutter counties in other ways as well. Two notorious killers operated in the area, Joaquin Murieta in the early 1850s and Juan Corona in 1971.

The legendary Murieta terrorized the Gold Rush mining camps. Acting on a tip that Murieta was camped at Sonorian Camp, Sheriff R.B. Buchanan organized a posse but was ambushed and shot. After he had been dragged three miles back to town and given up for

A 100-foot long Chinese dragon entertains an ethnic Yuba City and Marysville crowd in 1930. Courtesy, California State Library

lower rates whenever possible. Nonetheless, white Americans resented this practice, which they considered as taking jobs away from themselves, the "rightful" employees.

With political power and weaponry in the hands of whites, the Chinese were forcibly eliminated from labor and commerce. In Nicolaus angry white residents organized to export all Chinese laborers by boat to San Francisco. In Chico a Chinese settlement was burned. In Los Angeles, in 1871, whites massacred their Chinese neighbors.

Orientals in general were regarded as a threat to the posture of white su-

dead, it turned out that the bullet had passed safely through his breast, and he recovered.

More recently, Juan Corona was convicted of filling a mass grave with 25 farm laborers in his employ. The brutal 1971 crime involved multiple stabbings and machete blows. Corona, eligible for parole since 1982 under existing court procedures, is appealing his conviction.

A far less lethal criminal, Black Bart, gentleman bandit of the foothills, wrote hold-up demands in verse, carried an empty gun, and killed no one. Captured in 1883 by Wells Fargo officials, the out-law, whose real name was Charles Bolles, spent five years at San Quentin, then returned to Yuba County to claim the woman he had courted at Woodville (now Woodleaf). Black Bart kept a rented room in Marysville during his eight years of stage robbery. In 1955 a flood would reveal an escape tunnel through the le-vee from this room.

Labor disputes would also mar the region. Early in the twentieth century, agriculture underwent industrialization at the Durst Ranch in Wheatland. Unlike automobile assembly, mass production of a crop, which is perishable, requires

The Gong family of Marysville posed for this formal portrait, probably around the turn of the century. The Chinese cul-ture, typified by this family's appearance, went unnoticed by the ''pure'' Ameri-cans dominating the social structure. Courtesy, California State Library and Sacramento Museum and History Division

Many migrants, unable to afford the company tent rental, slept between the hops at night. Courtesy, Orrin Rounds and Special Collections, Meriam Library, California State University, Chico

strict timing. At Durst the single crop was hops.

In order to ensure sufficient labor at low cost, owner Ralph H. Durst promised work to all who would apply by August 1, with bonuses for staying through the season. Twenty-eight hundred workers arrived to harvest a crop requiring only 1,500. Furthermore, hops were weighed at day's end when they had dried out and their weight was at a minimum.

As was typical with employers of migratory labor, Durst Ranch erected minimal facilities for workers. Company-owned tents rented for 75 cents a week; nine toilets, located a mile from camp, served all 2,800 residents. The toilets were also used for dumping garbage. Although no water was provided for workers in the over 100-degree temperatures, a concessionaire sold citric acid "lemonade" at five cents a glass.

As a result of these conditions, the garbage piles bred flies and maggots; dysentery, typhoid, and malaria broke out; and workers who elsewhere could earn $4 a day were managing to collect between 70 cents and $1.90.

This one-of-a-kind booth was used at the county fairs of the 1920s by the Marysville *Appeal*. Its rivalry with the other leading newspaper in the area, the *Democrat*, ended with a merger in 1927. Today the *Appeal-Democrat* is the leading daily in the Twin Cities area. Courtesy, Sacramento History Center

Any attempt by the workers to organize met with strong opposition. Then, as now, any intimation of "communism" had the capacity to render otherwise sane citizens witless. Newspapers sensationalized the "communist conspiracy" charge leveled against Industrial Workers of the World (IWW).

In fact, Durst's workers numbered fewer than 30 IWW members. Dissatisfaction among Durst's employees reached a point, however, that with IWW members as spokesmen, they announced a decision to leave the ranch en masse by the following Sunday unless "high polers" were engaged to lift down the vines and a pay raise granted. Durst refused and the strike began.

Meanwhile, newspapers queried the management, and a statement was issued by accountant Murray Durst, Ralph's brother. The ranch furnished firewood, straw, city and well water, and ice water on the job, said he. Poor workers were grubstaked by the company for the first day and were subsequently paid three times a day. Furthermore, he claimed, 90 percent of the receipts went to workers.

During the negotiations, a police-

man arrived in order to arrest the IWW spokesmen but failed because he in fact had no warrant. The meeting returned to order, but a posse waiting outside roared in with clubs and guns. Four men died in the raid. Among them were District Attorney Ray Manwell and an unidentified Puerto Rican laborer who had struck the sheriff.

One hundred workers were arrested and denied representation. They were beaten and deprived of sleep until they "confessed." The charge was upped from "participation in a riot" to murder, without prospect of bail.

Of the four defendants left at trial time, two were convicted, two acquitted. No worker served on the jury, since none qualified as a property owner.

A Marysville *Democrat* editorial called the IWW members "venomous human snakes preaching the religion of hate, and their weapons are always destruction of property. The lives of two brave officers have been sacrificed. How long will a civilized community permit them to exist?"

Only the *Sacramento Bee*, in an article with the by-line of James McClatchy, reported anything other than the company statement.

The Congregational Church of Marysville questioned local news coverage and appointed a committee to investigate workers' claims. Governor Hiram Johnson appointed a Commission on Immigration and Industry to investigate migratory worker conditions, and the Federal Commission on Industrial Relations was formed.

The latter determined that the IWW was harmful to the war effort and unpatriotic. Meanwhile, the investigations had revealed deplorable working conditions, and Durst Ranch cooperated in setting up a model labor camp in 1914.

Agricultural advances were well underway in time to supply food for the soldiers who fought World War I. Farmers across the United States, mobilized by patriotism—and desire for profit—planted more crops than ever before. This war, which would inflame the national character with great sentimentality and high purpose, would yet wreak havoc upon the land.

After years of overplanting, worsened by drought, the depleted soil dried up and drifted away. Farmers from the South and the Midwest stacked their household belongings and their young ones atop trucks and headed west. Some families rode the rails; some hitched auto rides on the highways. All sought work. The great river valleys of Northern California seemed like paradise to the drought-ridden refugees.

The Women's Civic Improvement Club of Marysville had long been preserving the beauty of the area. In 1904

Above: Armies of migrant workers sought continuous employment by following crop harvests from county to county and state to state. Single crop "factory agriculture" depersonalized the labor force and led to abuses and discontent. This tent city for workers was erected at the Durst Ranch in Wheatland for the hop harvest of 1913. Courtesy, Orrin Rounds and Meriam Library, California State University, Chico

World War I veterans re-created a mobilized foxhole for a 1922 parade. Photo by Henry Sackrider. Courtesy, California State Library

they hired John McClaren of Golden Gate Park fame to design Ellis Lake. The first tourists to arrive in Yuba City and Marysville by automobile in the 1920s were accommodated by auto courts. The Improvement Club added tents, showers, and a night guard for the comfort and convenience of visitors. Word of this hospitality spread nationwide, and other communities designed similar oases for weary tourists.

"Okies" and "Arkies," however,

were not considered tourists. The welcome mat was whisked away at the first sign of deprivation and poverty. Furthermore, as a source of cheap labor the migrants replaced the Chinese, Mexicans, Filipinos, and Hindustani as the alleged cause of economic distress and focus for

This family is representative of the steady and industrious farmers in Yuba County around the turn of the century. By 1905, the year this picture was taken, farmers in Yuba and Sutter counties were among the leaders in the state for orchard, row, and rice crops. Courtesy, Sacramento History Center

In 1922 Kaffen's Grill offered fine dining in a setting which included snowy white linens, potted plants, private booths, and a player piano. Photo by Henry Sackrider. Courtesy, California State Library

bitter resentment. Destitute migrants lined river banks and ditches and their hungry children swelled the schools, while a prosperous, insulated community shuddered at the spectre of homeless hordes.

Not until 1935 was State Emergency Relief available. An experimental government labor camp was set up in Marysville on Simpson Lane, alongside the river, with cottonwoods for shade, showers, toilets, and tent platforms.

Resettlement began in 1937. A father-and-son team, Cline and Donald Bull, bought up 20,000 acres of land south of the Yuba River and offered it for sale to Caucasians. Their charge was $200 an acre at 6 percent. Many migrants settled in the town of Olivehurst, where their families remain today. As irrigation expanded and opened new land

The Lou K. Newfield house at 540 B Street in Yuba City typified the realization of the American dream in 1927, just before the Great Depression struck. Photo by Henry Sackrider. Courtesy, California State Library

In 1930 the National Theatre, "Home of the Talkies," featured Hoot Gibson and Winnie Lightner. At that time E Street in Marysville was wide and tree-lined with a park-like divider, fulfilling the gracious promise of the original town plan. Courtesy, California State Library

to cultivation, some eventually prospered at farming and ranching.

Altering the 100-year interval predicted by W.T. Ellis, two floods rivaling the inundation of 1861 to 1862 occurred in the north valley in 1955 and 1986.

The swollen Feather River tore a 2,200-foot gap in the levee at Shanghai Bend just below Yuba City on Christmas Eve, 1955. Water sped through to the by-pass levee and then swirled back to flood Yuba City and the surrounding 150 square miles, except for Marysville. Thirty-eight lives and many homes were lost.

That year Marysville was spared. William T. Ellis, who had spent his life

American Indians found employment in agriculture after their displacement by white settlers and gold seekers. This family, photographed in 1950, had not completely adopted the life-style of the white man. Courtesy, *Sacramento Bee* and Sacramento Museum and History Division

building the levee system, had died three months earlier. He was buried on the levee in a grave marked by his warning, "Always watch the tricky Yuba."

The levee break of 1986 which flooded Olivehurst and Linda left thousands homeless, and although many animals died, miraculously, no human lives were lost.

During the momentous cultural changes of the 1960s, a different sort of demolition took place in Marysville. Buildings of historic significance and sturdy construction, huge shade trees and parks, all immune to floods, fell instead to wrecking crews. City officials, in a rash of efficiency, competition, and "progress," traded away the aesthetic charm, beauty, and character of their community.

Glass brick and broad, unrelieved walls of stucco took the place of historic Cortez Square and the state fair pavilion. Ancient trees were leveled and gardens razed. Brick buildings tumbled, and contractors from more enlightened cities bought up the artifacts. Too late would Marysville's own citizens recognize their value.

This photograph of Feather River flooding was made by Merrit Nickerson for the California Department of Transportation in 1940. Courtesy, Sacramento Museum and History Division

Construction of a second Feather River bridge at Tenth Street in the 1950s eased the traffic burden between Yuba City and Marysville. City officials are shown inspecting the progress. Courtesy, Special Collections, Meriam Library, California State University, Chico, and Community Memorial Museum, Sutter County

CHAPTER VI

MODULATION

A bird's-eye view taken today from the sky above Yuba County's airport offers a vastly changed perspective of the north valley. Less than 200 years ago travelers spent weeks coming down from the Sierra Nevada and days walking the valley within sight of the Buttes. Present-day speed and technology have rendered time brief and distance slight. Jet streams of Beale Air Force Base traffic stripe the sky. River transport, which only recently offered the quickest route, has become obsolete.

Flying north from Olivehurst, one soon catches sight of the broad rectangle of the Yuba Community College compound, with its experimental farm plots and aggregation of buildings.

Marysville lies north across the Yuba River where it meets the Feather. The bird's-eye view of the cityscape and river confluence has not changed much since the 1870s. A prominent feature remains the tower of St. Joseph's Church. The fine old tree-shaded, river-front plaza where Cordua's Adobe stood rests buried under the levee. Technology has

The land of the Sutter Buttes retains much of its early character where reclamation and factory farming have not intruded. Photo by Ron Sanford

The Hart Building of Marysville greets travelers crossing the Yuba River on State Highway 70. Refurbished in 1984, this landmark houses office suites. Photo by David Parker. Courtesy, *Appeal-Democrat*

left its imprint, however. Today bridges cross the Yuba for trains and automobiles, and the sharp angle between the rivers now shelters sewage treatment ponds.

Orchards ripen alongside the Yuba River on land recovered 100 years after hydraulic mining took its toll. Further east the Yuba Goldfields' operations fill the river bottom, which crosses the flight path at Beale Air Force Base. Min-

ing continues by dredger, with deep blue ponds and long symmetrical mounds marking the riverbed past Park's Bar Bridge on Highway 20. Timbuctoo lies near Smartsville, its hillsides similarly scarred by hydraulics.

A large dam forms Englebright Reservoir. Boats are docked at the marina and, upriver, white streaks trailed by water-skiers skim the blue surface. Further east the river narrows into

The Yuba River (foreground) enters the Feather River near Marysville's sewage treatment ponds. Yuba City lies beyond the Feather River to the right. Photo by David Giles

According to ecologists, the lumber industry practice of clear-cutting timber causes erosion and destroys forests and wildlife habitats for generations. Oregon Hill in Yuba County is one place where this has occurred. Photo by David Giles

ever deepening canyons. Near Dobbins the Colgate Power Plant hugs the water at the foot of a great conduit over the mountain. The Yuba's north fork is dammed at Bullard's Bar; its reservoir spreads miles up the canyons, nearly to Camptonville, and reaches into the Plumas and Tahoe national forests.

Forests peaked with fir, spruce, cedar, and pine cover the rugged terrain. Black oak grows sparsely among the timber, much of it having been harvested for fuel or removed by logging operations. Occasionally a mountaintop lies bald, streaked with erosion gulleys tracked by clear-cutting.

Southwest, at lower elevations, more man-made lakes appear: Lake Francis at Dobbins; Lake Mildred at Thousand Trails Recreation Area; and various ponds at the Renaissance community of the Fellowship of Friends. Three hundred sixty-five acres of vineyard cover Renaissance's groomed hills.

Flying north of the Collins Lake Recreation Area at Stanfield Hill, one views Honcut Creek as it forms the border with Butte County. Oak-studded rolling hills and cattle ranches distinguish Loma Rica. Heading west, the land flattens and grows greener, its geometric pattern of property lines occasionally relieved by the curve of wandering creekbeds. The Buttes rise up in the west, and beyond them, beyond Colusa County, appears the innermost coastal range.

As one approaches the Buttes, farms give way to marshes and duck hunting clubs among the rivers. Butte Sink is as yet sparsely settled; round patches of tule remain where rice has yet to intrude.

Protections are in place in these regions to guard the water fowls' natural habitat. Herons still fly along the winding surface of a creek, sharply outlined against water sometimes glittering, sometimes shadowed by brush and trees.

Butte Creek flows down the valley west of the Buttes to meet the Sacramento River above Meridian. When one looks around the Buttes to the east, Yuba City comes into view across the Sutter Bypass. A patchwork of variegated farmlands stretches across the landscape, with the Sacramento River twisting wildly in loops and streamers of smooth blue ribbon.

Across the river from Knight's Landing, tall grain elevators rise, glowing amber in the late afternoon sunlight. The Sacramento carves a last broad curve there before it meets the Feather at Verona.

The town of Vernon, where the Kanakas once grew taro and gathered at evening to play their ukuleles, has disappeared. Here is the southernmost point of both Sutter and Yuba counties; Yolo and Sacramento counties lie beyond the rivers. When one returns north along the Feather River past Nicolaus toward Marysville, the unprepossessing Bear River, almost hidden in the brush, empties into the Feather west of Wheatland.

The Russian fur-trading center of Fort Ross, which John Sutter purchased long ago, lies due west in the path of the setting sun. The old buildings there have been restored by the State of California Department of Parks and Recreation, with minimal alterations to their original setting. Late in life Sutter expressed regret that he had not built his retreat on that barren shoreline of heavy fog and thin soil.

The geographic contours of Yuba and Sutter counties, although undergoing change from geologic disturbance, are no longer being disrupted by mining. Sutter County lies in the valley at sea level. About half of Yuba County's 637 square miles is flatland; the other half rises into the Sierra foothills to a height of about 4,000 feet.

Agriculture dominates the Yuba County economy, with crop values ranging in 1986 from $13 million for rice to

SUTTER and YUBA COUNTIES
1850~1950

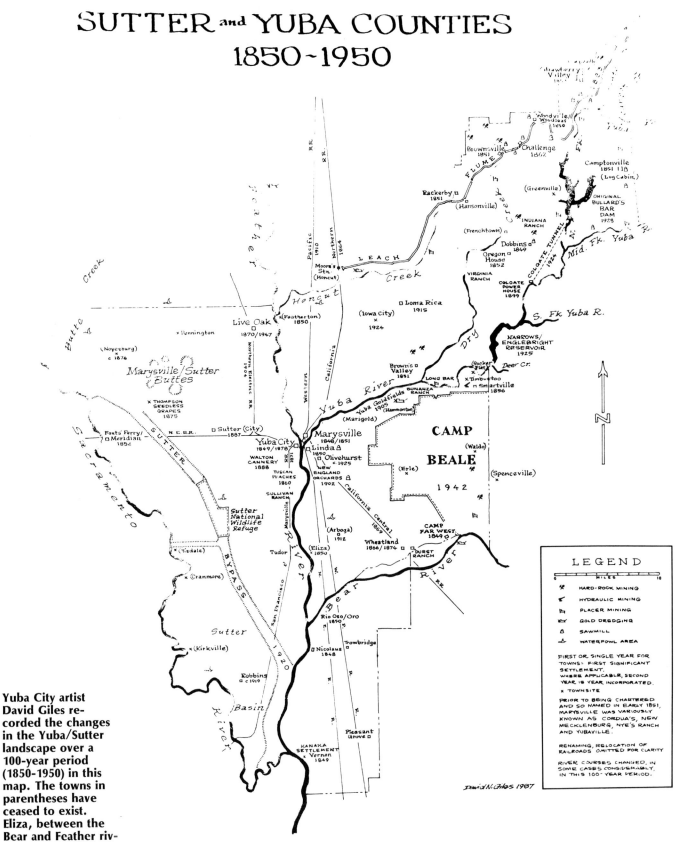

Yuba City artist David Giles recorded the changes in the Yuba/Sutter landscape over a 100-year period (1850-1950) in this map. The towns in parentheses have ceased to exist. Eliza, between the Bear and Feather rivers, was established by Captain Sutter to honor his only daughter.

LEGEND

MILES 0 ———— 10

⚒ HARD-ROCK MINING
⚒ HYDRAULIC MINING
⚒ PLACER MINING
⚒ GOLD DREDGING
⚒ SAWMILL
⚒ WATERFOWL AREA

FIRST OR SINGLE YEAR FOR TOWNS: FIRST SIGNIFICANT SETTLEMENT.
WHERE APPLICABLE, SECOND YEAR IS YEAR INCORPORATED.
X TOWNSITE

PRIOR TO BEING CHARTERED AND SO NAMED IN EARLY 1851, MARYSVILLE WAS VARIOUSLY KNOWN AS CORDUA'S, NEW MECKLENBURG, NYE'S RANCH AND YUBAVILLE.

RENAMING, RELOCATION OF RAILROADS OMITTED FOR CLARITY

RIVER COURSES CHANGED, IN SOME CASES CONSIDERABLY, IN THIS 100-YEAR PERIOD.

David N. Giles 1987

The moon rises over the steep face of South Butte in Sutter County. Photo by Walt Anderson

Right: Almond blossoms arch overhead in a display which extends for acres upon acres through the Yuba-Sutter region. Photo by Walt Anderson

Above: This juxtaposition of dogwood and madrone trees illustrates the intricacy of nature. Photo by John Hendrickson

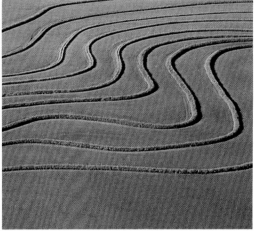

Above: Seeded from the air in the spring, contoured fields of rice darken to emerald green under a hot summer sun. Photo by Ron Sanford

Pickups halted in their tracks along La Porte Stage Road early one morning at the sight of this colorful display at Sun Dog Ranch. Artist Jerry Egan and friends arranged this example of conceptual art, altering beholder concepts of beauty. Photo by Vance Dickinson

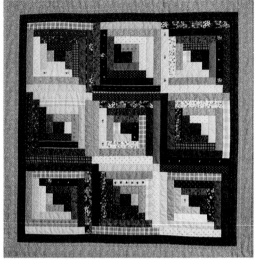

Above: "Log Cabin, Straight Furrows," is the title of Candace Head's quilt portraying her impressions of the Yuba-Sutter landscape. The Loma Rica artist won Best of Show and first prize in the 1987 conference of the American/International Quilt Association, and earned the title of Master Quilter. Photo by David Giles. Courtesy, Mary E. McClain

Above: Tall blue stands of bush lupine, interspersed with bright orange California poppies and the shiny red foliage of poison oak, line roads throughout the Yuba foothills. Photo by Walt Anderson

Boy Scout Troop 21 races along the Feather River toward the finish line during a weekend campout in Marysville's Riverfront Park. Photo by Dave Nielsen

The Sutter County Courthouse was built in 1858, but was destroyed by fires in 1871 and 1899. This replica of the original has classic lines with an Italian influence. A Victorian cupola was added at the top. Photo by James Wurschmidt

The Marysville Stampede brings ranchers, cowboys, and spectators to Riverfront Park each May for the home performance of Cotton Rosser's Flying U Rodeo. Contestants train for major events at practice arenas throughout the flatlands and foothills. Photo by Dave Nielsen. Courtesy, *Appeal-Democrat*

Mechanical sails revolved in the wind to power pumps, millstones, and saws for Yuba-Sutter pioneers. This one, silhouetted at sunset, probably still pumps water. Photo by Walt Anderson

Foothills artist Jack Thodt decorated the ceiling of a roadside dive, The Last Outpost, with scenes from local history. The Last Outpost is located near Forbestown, on the border between Yuba and Butte counties. Photo by Dave Nielsen. Courtesy, *Appeal-Democrat*

$1.3 million for corn. Other agricultural commodities in descending order of value are prunes, peaches, walnuts, cattle, kiwi, milk, pears, pasture, timber, wild rice, and almonds.

Employment in the combined counties, with a population over 100,000, is charted by job categories for 1986 as follows:

Agriculture	*3,625*
Mining/Construction	*1,475*
Manufacturing	*2,650*
Food/Related	*800*
Lumber/Wood	*950*
Other manufacturing	*900*
Transportation/Utilities	*1,375*
Wholesale trade	*1,200*
Retail trade	*6,350*
Finance/Real estate	*1,375*
Services	*5,375*
Federal Government	*1,450*
State Government	*850*
Local Gov't/Education	*5,800*

Below: This young girl finds refreshment at Riverfront Park, which lies along the Feather River between Yuba City and Marysville. A large open amphitheater attracts summer crowds to concerts and celebrations, and camping and fishing facilities are nearby. Photo by Dave Nielsen. Courtesy, *Appeal-Democrat*

Members of an official delegation from Peikang, Taiwan, sister city to Marysville, proudly wave their national flags at the 106th Bok Kai parade in 1986. The Bok Kai parade is held each spring in honor of the Chinese water god, who controls rivers, floods, and rains. Courtesy, *Appeal-Democrat*

California unemployment figures matched the national rate of 6.7 percent in December 1986. Unemployment in Yuba and Sutter counties measured 16.3 percent at that time.

In order to facilitate a healthy business climate, certain civic organizations are attempting to correct a cash-flow deprivation.

Another group of civic-minded individuals is eager to preserve the natural beauty of the region. This faction focuses on the rescue and restoration of fine architecture, parks, and trees.

The serene environment and mild winters of Yuba and Sutter counties meanwhile attract transients, immigrants, and seasonal workers—who require housing and public assistance.

Meanwhile wildlife associations and hunters are beginning to recognize a common goal in maintaining a natural habitat for game survival. The California Department of Fish and Game proposes to establish an 87-acre wildlife refuge in

the floodplains of the Yuba and Feather rivers and the Jack Slough, with riparian forests and marshes maintained as sanctuaries.

The Yuba County-Sutter County Regional Arts Council is a major cohesive force as it unites the two counties in revitalizing the economy through the arts. Whereas ethnic chauvinism once divided the communities, the Regional Arts Council promotes a richly diverse cultural and artistic heritage within Yuba and Sutter counties. Maidu Indians, East Indians, Orientals, Asians, Africans, Mexicans, Greeks, and Filipinos are all rediscovering appreciation for their gifts.

The annual spring Bok Kai Festival brings religious pilgrims of Chinese descent to Marysville to venerate the river god at his only temple in the western hemisphere. The Bok Kai Festival is in its eleventh decade.

Uniting commercial and artistic resources to bolster the local economy, the first annual Prune Festival of Yuba and Sutter counties will take place in September 1988. Having been relegated to last place (number 329) in a Rand-McNally Corporation 1986 rating of places to live, the region good-naturedly responds by celebrating prunes. Paraphrasing author Shel Silverstein, the Yuba City prune "may look wrinkled and wet, and withered," but it is an agent of health nonetheless.

With autumn festivals in the flatlands and the spring Bok Kai ceremonies at the Yuba-Feather river confluence, midsummer draws visitors up into the cool foothills. The Yuba-Feather Medical Center sponsors a Mountain Fair during the first weekend in July, featuring contests and a regional art exhibition. In winter, cross-country skiing and holiday craft sales attract tourists to the high country.

The Sikh Temple Guirdwara Yuba City receives worshipers and visitors from throughout the United States. Sikhs began migrating to Sutter County in 1916, finding a climate and terrain comparable to their native state of Punjab. The entire community is invited to a parade and celebration in November,

when the white swans first arrive, to honor the coronation of the holy scripture, *Granth Sahib.*

Another event held in November, organized by the Greek community, is a weekend of celebration and dancing, featuring the partaking of homeland delicacies.

Appreciation Day opens Beale Air Force Base to visitors for air shows, demonstrations, and informational tours of state-of-the-art aircraft. Beale accounts for 14 percent of the Yuba County population.

A popular Japanese holiday, the Obon Festival, is sponsored by the Buddhist Church in mid-July and is open to the community at large. Traditional dances are performed during the festival, and taiko drums and teriyaki dinners draw cosmopolitan crowds.

After the close of the U.S. involvement in the wars in Southeast Asia in

Advanced music students form the Yuba College Chamber Singers, under the direction of Joaquina Johnson, seated in the front row, far right. Many music and drama students from Yuba College are earning recognition as performing artists. Photo by Barry Gumm. Courtesy, Yuba Community College

Businesspeople and professionals in Yuba and Sutter counties find that exercise and competition offer a welcome release after a day in the office. Health clubs and team sports revive flagging spirits and bodies. Photo by David Parker

Below: ''Bobby Fischer Eyes'' won an award for *Appeal-Democrat* photographer Dave Nielsen, who captured this strategist at work during a chess exhibition at Peach Tree Mall in Linda.

1975, refugees from Vietnam and Cambodia began arriving in Yuba and Sutter counties under relocation programs. With them they brought a wealth of resources. Chief among these are fabric arts and fine handwork.

Yuba Community College, Beale Air Force Base, and the Regional Arts Council all sponsor ethnic entertainments. The fine arts are performed in schools and auditoriums or displayed in public and professional buildings. For example, the Tri-county Community Concert Association series regularly draws full houses for the Marysville Auditorium.

Meanwhile, new construction reflects a returning emphasis upon aesthetics. Planning commissions are adding requirements for landscaping and shade trees.

Several theater arts presentations are offered each year at the Yuba College Theatre. The theater hosted the national premier of a play by Nobel-prize winner Elie Wiesel; and a Yuba College production, *Of Mice and Men,* was one of six finalists in the 1987 American College Theatre Festival.

The professional quality of the Yuba College Symphony Chorus has evolved to a level of joint performance of major choral works with the Sacramento Symphony.

Churches throughout the area con-

tinue to cultivate the tradition of sacred music. Notable among their offerings is St. Isidore's yearly Christmas sponsorship of the *Messiah,* performed by the Yuba Sutter Oratorio Society. Chamber music ensembles and arts exhibitions are variously scheduled at the Sutter Community Memorial Museum.

Meanwhile tourists are discovering the exceptional natural beauty and recreational resources long noted by historians, artists, and writers. The mild climate, clean air, rivers, waterfowl, mountains, and open spaces also attract a diverse collection of retirees and free-spirited fugitives from the madding corporate crowd.

In 1986 three-year-old Shree Kelly was the youngest member of the Mt. Olivet Baptist Church Choir. A spiritual songfest opened Black Awareness Week at Yuba Community College in that year, with choirs from Beale Air Force Base, Christ Temple Community Church, and Bethel AME singing gospel and secular music. Photo by David Parker. Courtesy, *Appeal-Democrat*

Geese safely obey traffic signals, crossing D Street on their way to Ellis Lake in Marysville on a wet and stormy January day in 1986. Photo by David Parker. Courtesy, *Appeal-Democrat*

Clara Sheldon Smith, whose family later operated a silent movie theater in Marysville, photographed the Marysville Fire Department in 1901. Courtesy, Marysville Fire Department and Sacramento Museum and History Division

CHAPTER VII

PARTNERS IN PROGRESS

Those first few glittering flakes of gold discovered by John Marshall in 1848 echoed a promise that drew thousands from all over the world to what would become Yuba and Sutter counties. It was an area, prior to the Gold Rush, populated by only a few white settlers, fur trappers, and thousands of Indians, and considered so desolate that it was overlooked by early Spanish padres and Mexican officials.

The argonauts came, and along with them men who saw beyond the taking of gold nuggets to a greater wealth. They were the men who saw profit in trading with the ill-equipped miners; farmers who saw rich soil, clear waters, and a mild climate; and the professionals who saw opportunity—lawyers, doctors, newspapermen. These were the individuals who would settle the area.

Yuba City was laid out before Marysville, in anticipation of catching the trade of miners headed north, but fate placed the town, built on an Indian village, on the wrong side of the river. Ship captains opted to land at a place across the river that would become Marysville—a natural terminus that was soon the major supply center for the northern mines.

Marysville developed rapidly, and by 1853 was the third-largest city in California. It was called the Hub City, as almost all roads to the mines radiated from it. Day and night stages, wagons,

and pack trains charged through the streets, and ships and stages arrived and departed many times a day. There were hotels, saloons, lumber companies, brickyards, steam sawmills, stores, and a variety of services. A daily newspaper grew from a semi-weekly started in 1950.

Marysville built the first public library west of the Mississippi River, became the site of the first state fair, and saw its first alcalde, Stephen J. Field, named to the U.S. Supreme Court as the first western appointee. Frederick Low, the first California governor to serve a four-year term, was from Marysville, as was Charles E. DeLong, the first western minister to Japan.

Yuba City was growing, too, as a farming community. The rich alluvial soil produced abundant crops. Wheat was first grown in 1850, and soon vegetables, fruits, and nuts were raised. Peaches proved such a good and profitable crop that eventually Yuba City was named the Peach Bowl of the World. In 1913 rice was first grown commercially, and still ranks high in importance. Most recently, prunes have surpassed peaches; the region is now the world's largest prune-producing area in the world. The vast agricultural enterprise of Sutter County has also provided a wealth of related industries—canneries, processing plants, and mills employ thousands of people.

Developing the area was not easy. There were many obstacles to overcome, and it took vigorous men and women to drain the fields, build bypasses and levees, and rebuild after the towns were ravaged by fires and floods. But, unlike other Gold Rush towns, those in Yuba and Sutter grew and prospered.

The organizations whose stories are detailed on the following pages have chosen to support this important literary and civic project. They illustrate the variety of ways in which individuals and businesses have contributed to the growth and development of Yuba and Sutter counties.

YUBA/SUTTER REGIONAL ARTS COUNCIL

The Yuba/Sutter Regional Arts Council, the first regional arts council in the state, was established through merger in September 1986 as a result of the two counties' desire to accomplish more effective arts planning, provide a wider base of support for the arts, and to strengthen existing arts organizations. In pooling their talents and resources they have endowed their collective communities with a rich climate of creative accomplishment.

"The Yuba/Sutter Regional Arts Council is a unique and successful blend of two counties' art resources, a very active rural partner . . . one of the best in the state," says Robert Reid, executive director of the California Arts Council.

Lee Burrows, executive director of YSRAC, says that since it began, the council has grown to approximately 1,000 members, whose dues provide more than 10 percent of the revenue for programs.

In order to promote art awareness and participation from the

Lee Burrows, executive director of the Yuba/Sutter Regional Arts Council.

Some of the board members at the time the two art councils merged were (left to right): Dr. Paul Cohen, Joaquina Johnson, Bob Laddish, Don Huckins, Katherine Lauppe, June Sheffield, Erna Barnickol, Steve Cantrell, and Marnie Crowhurst.

community, a variety of programs are offered. For example, the Arts In Education project, directed by Mark McCrary, associate director of YSRAC, places qualified artists in schools to teach local children everything from puppetmaking to origami. Patty Martin even conducts courses in theater exercise and sign language.

"Arts in Education is one of the most important things we do, because it offers children the chance to create . . . not necessarily to become professional artists, but to become individual people," says McCrary.

Another important program is Arts in Public Places, which gives local artists an opportunity to display their work, on a rotating basis, at various commercial and civic locations. Lillian Bowmer developed this program now held in 20 locations.

Annual events presented by YSRAC include the Very Special

Arts Festival, featuring exhibits and performances by disabled children and adults; the Discovery Trails Art Tour in the foothills; and the Light Opera Gala.

Bringing performing arts to the community is also in the purview of the YSRAC's community service. Visiting dance troupes and musical groups have included the Oakland Ballet, Donald Pippin and the San Francisco Pocket Opera, the San Francisco Theatre Ballet, and world-class pianist Istvan Nadas.

Through these events, says Burrows, "we bring quality programs that people may not otherwise be exposed to in a small, rural community."

The YSRAC also publishes a bimonthly newsletter and the *Artists Registry/Directory*. With Continental Cablevision YSRAC coproduces "Artists Alive," a weekly showcase for local talent, as well as touring artists.

"Art comes to you proposing, frankly, to give nothing but the highest quality to your moments," wrote Walter Pater in 1873. Taking these words to heart, the Yuba/Sutter Regional Arts Council is providing some of those moments to the citizens of its community.

SUNSET MOULDING CO., INC.

When Gayle Morrison returned to his home in Yuba City in 1945, discharged from the U.S. Army Air Corps, he found that his brother and father had started a small sawmill at Challenge in the Yuba foothills. With the eye of an entrepreneur, he saw there was a need for a concentration yard where the rough lumber from the small mills could be dried, surfaced, and milled to pattern before being sold. By the end of 1945 he opened a yard—Yuba City Planing Mill and Lumber Co., where he and six employees planed, hand-stacked, air-dried, and remanufactured lumber that was then sold to two distribution centers in Los Angeles.

Morrison and his wife, Meredith—they had married that year—planned and worked together. She kept the books, and they also farmed 200 acres—"mostly at night."

In July 1948 Morrison formed a partnership with two brothers, Buford and Carl Williams, and founded Sunset Moulding Co., Inc. It was located on Live Oak Highway, eight miles north of Yuba City, where it remains today. Morrison ran both the planing mill and Sunset until 1950, when he closed the planing mill to concentrate his efforts on the fast-growing Sunset Moulding Co.

In 1974 he bought out the Williams brothers, and Sunset became a family-owned business, except for Ken Olson, a key employee who had joined the firm in 1959. Olson was named vice-president of Sunset in 1974.

Five years later Sunset acquired three additional manufacturing facilities. By 1980 plants were opened at Susanville, Cottonwood, and in Rocklin, where Morrison Building Materials, Inc., was established.

The Morrison children took an early interest in the business and

Meredith (left) and Gayle Morrison. When Sunset Moulding started in 1948, Meredith kept the books and Gayle ran the company. Today the firm and its subsidiaries employ 335 workers, including a staff of 20 for Sunset's record keeping.

were often included in "shop talk." The two boys worked after school and during summer vacations while they attended high school and college. Ric, the oldest, joined the firm in 1969, and later became president of Sun Forest, Inc., which is a sales arm of Sunset. John joined the firm in 1980, and he is now vice-president of Morrison Building Materials. Daughter Linda Morrison Talbert joined the firm in 1986, and works in the main office and the accounting department.

Sunset Moulding has come a long way since it was started in 1948. Meredith Morrison used to keep the company books on her kitchen table. Today a staff of 20, with completely computerized facilities, handles the record keeping. Sunset Moulding and its subsidiaries employ 335 workers. The Yuba City plant averages 200 employees, and is one of the largest manufacturing companies in the Yuba-Sutter area.

Gayle Morrison is active in the community and has won numerous awards for his many activities. He serves on the boards of both Fremont and Rideout hospitals and is past president of Rotary, which granted him the Employer of the Year Award in 1986, and the Paul Harris Award. The E.D.D. named him Veteran's Advocate of 1987.

When young Gayle Morrison, as a bomber pilot, flew hundreds of miles in a badly damaged B-24 to bring his men back to safety, he showed courage, intelligence, and determination—qualities that he carried into the business world, and that have made him successful. His efforts have benefited hundreds of people, and contribute much to the community.

Sunset Moulding's board of directors (left to right): Linda Morrison Talbert, Ken Olson, Ric Morrison, John Morrison, and Gayle Morrison.

MARYSVILLE MEDICAL GROUP

In 1938 four physicians combined their private practices to form a multiservice medical group called the Marysville Medical Clinic. It was the first of such facilities in California and was patterned after the Mayo Clinic in Rochester, Minnesota.

Dr. Granville S. Delamere, who guided the project, completed his four-year residency there and returned to Marysville, where he set up his first practice on D Street in an office he shared with general practitioner Dr. John A. Duncan. When the city's first high rise, the Hart Building, was constructed, the two young doctors leased its top floor.

They soon became acquainted with Dr. Phillip E. Hoffman, whose specialty was obstetrics and gynecology, and Dr. Samuel Morris, a New York native who specialized in diseases of the eyes, ears, nose, and throat. The four physicians decided that by combining their diverse specialties in a single clinic, they could provide convenient care for their patients at a lower cost.

With a loan of $40,000, the clinic was built at the corner of Fourth and H streets. As the staff and services increased, other specialties were added, along with X-ray facilities, laboratory services, physical therapy, and a pharmacy. The building itself also went through many transformations, with additions made wherever possible to accommodate the clinic's rapid expansion.

Today, more than 50 years since the small medical facility was begun, the original concept of providing cost-efficient, quality health care at one location is still the premise on which the Marysville Medical Group is based. The partnership of physicians and professional corporations, with more than 50 highly trained, board-certified specialists, is one of the largest privately owned

The original Marysville Medical Clinic was located at the corner of Fourth and H streets. The facility had four doctors and 11 employees in 1938.

and administrated medical groups in Northern California. It is also one of the largest employers in the area.

In 1968 larger facilities were constructed at 800 Third Street. The two-story, award-winning structure is located on three acres, with 55,000 square feet of space and a 200-car parking lot. Completed in February 1968 at a cost of $1.2 million, the structure houses separate

This bronze plaque honoring the founding doctors of the Marysville Medical Group hangs in the main facility at 800 Third Street.

departments for medical treatment, and a physician from each department is on call 24 hours a day, seven days a week. Extensive diagnostic equipment includes advanced technology for X-ray, lab services, ultrasound, low-dose mammography, nuclear medicine, PUVA, and CT scan.

In 1985 further expansion was needed, and a unique center for women, children, and teens was built at 826 Fourth Street. Because women and children require very specific types of routine care and facilities, the doctors integrated their collective experience to develop a convenient, complete health care service.

The Marysville Medical Group acquired the Urgent Care Clinic in Yuba City in 1987. This immediate medical care facility for acute and minor emergency medical or surgical treatment is open seven days a week, from 8 a.m. to 8 p.m.

In 1987 MMG also acquired the Lincoln Medical Center, offering general medical care and related lab services, X-ray, and testing facilities.

Robert P. Ready, administrator of MMG, says, "The Marysville Medical Group will continue to strive for improved services to provide the best of health care for the community it serves . . ."

DR. ROBERT M. PEPPERCORN, M.D.

Dr. Robert Peppercorn opened his medical practice in Yuba City in 1983. He was new to the area, but soon established himself not only as a caring physician, but also as a man dedicated to community projects.

He chose Yuba City for the mild climate, natural beauty of the valley, and because he believed his many talents could be put to good use in a small, growing community.

Dr. Peppercorn was raised in Miami, Florida. His father was a dermatologist, his mother a registered nurse. When he was nine years old he received a tiny microscope, and set about examining everything that would fit on a slide. It was at that time he knew he wanted to be a doctor. He realized early that getting into medical school would not be easy, so he held two other career options—journalism and politics.

He was accepted at medical school, as an undergraduate at Harvard University, and as a graduate of Johns Hopkins Medical School in Baltimore in 1978. He interned at the University of Utah Medical Center in Salt Lake City in internal medicine, and from there attended Stanford University at Palo Alto for his residency in dermatology and allergy. By the time he finished his residency, he knew he wanted to stay in California. When an opening for a dermatologist in Marysville became available, he applied and was accepted. He stayed there for a year before going into practice for himself in Yuba City.

In 1983 Dr. Peppercorn became the writer, producer, and host of "The Medical Explorer," a medical information program seen twice weekly on Channel 5 cable television. He produced two guest interview programs for Channel 5, and then was asked to prepare a series that became "The Medical Explorer." Dr. Peppercorn enjoys the work involved in putting the show together. It has been running more

Dr. Peppercorn has contributed to the medical needs of the community since opening his practice in the Yuba City area in the early 1980s. In addition to being a recognized skin and allergy medical specialist, he writes and produces a television program, lectures at Stanford Medical School, and participates in a variety of civic programs.

than four years now and enjoys a wide audience.

A popular speaker, Dr. Peppercorn lectures at Stanford University, and also speaks locally to civic and community groups. His energy is boundless. He also supports the Yuba/Sutter Regional Arts Council, the chamber of commerce, and youth programs. He served as president of the Yuba-Sutter-Colusa County Medical Society, where he worked to provide more information to members about political candidates and issues affecting the medical profession.

His dream of a new building for his Skin and Allergy Medical

Group was completed in 1987 after two years of planning. The 4,000-square-foot facility at Shasta and Del Norte avenues in Yuba City incorporates the finest high-technology equipment available. The innovative design even includes a computerized teaching facility for patients. The Yuba City Planning Commission chose the building as the community's most outstanding new land development for 1987.

Another project important to Dr. Peppercorn is the establishment of a cash grant program for high school science students. Each month during 1988 he is awarding $150 to a deserving student selected by high school science instructors. The money can be used as the student pleases. Dr. Peppercorn believes that the early encouragement and recognition that he received were instrumental in his pursuit of a career in science. He hopes that his grant will give encouragement to some of the area's young people.

For Dr. Robert Peppercorn each day is filled with adventure, dedication, public service, and a desire to do everything well. His credo is simple: "I am what I do."

The Robert M. Peppercorn medical facility at Shasta and Del Norte avenues includes the finest high-technology equipment available for the treatment of the skin and allergies. The 4,000-square-foot building was named as the community's most outstanding new land development by the Yuba City Planning Commission in 1987.

HUNTLEY-SHEEHY INSURANCE CO., INC.

The history of Huntley-Sheehy Insurance Co. can be traced back to 1912, when Charles R. Boyd formed the Sutter Holding Company for the First National Bank of Yuba City.

Boyd was a Sutter County pioneer businessman and farmer who also belonged to the Farmers' Cooperative Union of Sutter County. The cooperative was established to process and merchandise crops, mainly hay and grain, grown by its members. At that time produce was shipped by boat down the Feather River from Yuba City to buyers in San Francisco. Boyd worked for the cooperative, first as a weigher, and eventually as manager.

To provide financial services for its members, the cooperative established the First National Bank of Yuba City in 1912, and named Charles R. Boyd as bank president. At that time he formed the Sutter Holding Company to handle insurance for the bank and its customers.

In 1926, when the Bank of Italy took control of First National, Sutter Holding became a separate and in-

Mal and Brad Huntley, present owners of Huntley-Sheehy Insurance, uphold the high standard set by the original company in 1912.

Mal and Brad Huntley outside the Huntley-Sheehy Insurance Company, located at 520 Olive Street in Marysville.

dependent insurance agency. C.R. Boyd appointed his son, Donald, as manager of the now-independent Sutter Holding Company. Donald Boyd was an experienced insurance agent who had worked for a number of years in San Francisco with the M. Thompson Company. Boyd was joined by his son-in-law, John J. Sheehy, in 1945.

In 1972 Sutter Holding Company merged with the prestigious Ellis-Huntley Company to form Huntley-Sheehy Insurance Co., Inc., with principals Mallard R. Huntley, Bradford Huntley, and John Sheehy.

The Ellis-Huntley firm had been established in 1924 by W.T. Ellis, Jr., who was considered by many to be Marysville's most respected citizen. Ellis was instrumental in stopping the devastating hydraulic mining in the foothills that filled the rivers with debris. He was also responsible for building a remarkable levee system that has, since it was completed, protected the city of Marysville from flood waters.

Raymond Huntley purchased the firm from Ellis in 1946, but kept the Ellis name out of respect for the man until his death in 1955. At the time he purchased the agency Ray Huntley had been the manager of the San Francisco branch of the Travelers Insurance Company.

In 1952 Ray Huntley sold one-half of the agency to his cousin Mal J. Huntley, who was at that time chief underwriting officer of a subsidiary of the Home Insurance company in the midwest.

In 1963 Mal's sons, Brad K. and Mal R., joined the firm. After the deaths of the senior partners, Mal R. Huntley, Brad Huntley, and John Sheehy formed the new agency. Sheehy retired in 1984, but remained semi-active until 1986.

Huntley-Sheehy Insurance Co. provides general insurance services in Yuba and Sutter counties. The firm is located at 520 Olive Street in Marysville. It specializes in commercial services, and there are 10 employees in addition to the principals.

The owners continue the tradition started more than 75 years ago of not only providing business services, but also being active in community and civic affairs.

YUBA COMMUNITY COLLEGE DISTRICT

The year was 1927. An idea first conceived in 1911 by Marysville high school principal J.C. Ray had finally become a reality—Marysville Junior College, one of the first junior colleges in California, opened its doors to 67 students. It was located in the Marysville High School at Seventh and G streets, and operated under the guidance of the Marysville High School superintendent, Curtis E. Warren.

Overcrowding soon became a problem, and with classes being held in stairwells and hallways, it was evident that a larger facility was needed. In 1928 the college moved to 18th and B streets, at the site of the new high school. That year citizens formed the Yuba County Community College District—the first such district in California.

By 1937 a separate facility for Yuba College was built across the street from the high school on 18 acres of land at a cost of $60,000. The school contained six classrooms, an auditorium, and a few offices, and served an enrollment of 354 students. That year another first in California was accomplished when Yuba College formed its own bus transportation system for students living in outlying areas. The new buses—carrying students from Oroville, Yuba City, Colusa, Gridley, Live Oak, and Wheatland—rolled up to the front door of the newly expanded institution.

In 1946 a group of faculty members, concerned that the college would never take its rightful place in the community until it was no longer part of the Marysville High School system, petitioned for a total separation, which was accomplished in the 1950s when Yuba College became accredited by the Western College Association, an accreditation it still has today.

The college moved to its present location in Linda, just outside of Marysville, on October 1,

1962. Thirteen buildings were constructed on a 160-acre site, and by 1966 three dormitories had been added. In the early 1970s the Colusa Center was established, and in 1974 portions of Yolo, Lake, and Glen counties were added to the fast-growing college system. A center was built in Woodland in 1976, which now also includes a library and two science buildings, and the Lake County Center additions include a business building and a vocational training building.

Currently the student population of Yuba College district—covering 4,192 acres—exceeds 10,000, with 118 full-time faculty members,

19 administrative personnel, and 150 classified staff members. The district provides a wide variety of programs in addition to preparing students for transfer to a four-year college. Occupational, technical, and general education programs are offered, as well as a complete service for disabled students, a child care center, counseling center, special remedial classes, and English-as-a-second-language courses.

Dr. Patricia L. Wirth, Superintendent/President of Yuba College, says of the important role the college plays in the community, "I am pleased that we continue to move ahead in maintaining and upgrading programs and services for our students. We at Yuba College continue to set new goals for the future, always with the success of our students as our first consideration."

Early Yuba College facilities demonstrate the diversity of instruction.

SUNSWEET GROWERS INC.

Mention dried fruit and the name Sunsweet immediately springs to mind. After all, Sunsweet has been America's favorite brand of prune for more than 70 years. The grower-owned marketing cooperative, which takes its name from this famous brand, is the world's largest handler of dried tree fruits.

Virtually all prunes sold in the United States come from California, where the prime farmland of Sutter County, along with other portions of the Sacramento Valley, produces more than half the world's prune tonnage.

Yuba City is the heart of the dried fruit industry, and since 1975 has been the site of Sunsweet's gigantic processing and packing plant. With 19 acres under one roof, the facility is the world's largest prune-packing plant and one of the largest food-processing operations of any kind, anywhere.

The Sunsweet facility makes a significant contribution to the quality of life in the Yuba/Sutter area, and the prune orchards scattered about the valley provide a good

Yuba City's first Sunsweet plant was built in 1919 and was located at the corner of Craddock and B streets. Today the plant is known as the largest prune-packing facility in the world.

source of income for California farming families.

"Sunsweet is a driving economic force in this city and county, employing between 375 and 500 workers year round," confirms Sunsweet president Harold W. Jackson, who has been with the co-op since 1976. "It is also a major customer of the city from the standpoint of water purchase and property taxes," he adds.

The early days of September signal the beginning of the prune harvest, which lasts about a month. Most of the harvest is dehydrated at Sunsweet's drying plants, with 12 locations from Red Bluff to Madera. Sunsweet Dryers, a cooperative comprised of Sunsweet grower-members, dries prunes at a cost that is lower than that of independent dehydrators.

At the height of the season some 1,000 tons of dried prunes pass through the plant each day, and approximately 60,000 cases of prunes and other dried fruits are packed daily and stored in the shipping warehouse, which is nearly the size of three football fields. Approximately 96,000 gallons of juice—enough to fill up to 9,000 bottles an hour—flows through the plant's bottling lines. Through an agreement with Ocean Spray, Sunsweet

packs cranberry juice for that cooperative's West Coast market, and Ocean Spray packs Sunsweet juices for distribution on the East Coast.

The story of Sunsweet and the development of the California prune industry began in the Santa Clara Valley and nearby coastal regions. During the first 10 years of the twentieth century prune growers struggled for economic survival in glutted markets and were at the mercy of unscrupulous packers. Soon recognizing the need to band together, the growers organized California Prune and Apricot Growers, Inc., in 1917. This group comprised Sunsweet's predecessor, and chose San Jose as the site of its first headquarters and main offices, according to Dave Hannon, a 33-year veteran of Sunsweet. In 1919 the co-op purchased a warehouse at the corner of Craddock and B streets, and Yuba City had its first Sunsweet plant.

Despite the economic woes of the Great Depression, the association continued to promote the Sunsweet brand and was able to sell its crops at good prices, and further establish the Sunsweet brand. Prune juice, hailed as the most significant new product since dried fruit, was a boon to sales when it was added to the product line in 1932.

As the economy improved, new packing plants were built, and facilities modernized and expanded. In June 1950 the old Yuba City plant was sold, and Sunsweet constructed a larger building on Spiva Avenue. Postwar affluence brought changes in the marketplace—consumers had a greater choice of food items than ever before, and competition among food producers became keen. Labor also became scarce—as well as more costly—and Sunsweet engineers met the challenge by developing new labor-saving equipment to harvest and prepare the fruit for drying.

Harold W. Jackson, president of Sunsweet Growers Inc. since 1976.

Through the years Sunsweet has weathered many storms—both literally and figuratively. When torrential flooding in 1955 threatened the Yuba City plant, sandbags kept the facility's losses to a minimum. A few years later increased production, declining export markets, and decreased consumption of prunes presented another challenge to Sunsweet, which the firm answered with major marketing efforts. Then, in 1965, the company introduced a revolutionary, patented pitting machine, which increased sales of the new, pitted prunes.

In the meantime, many growers were selling their orchards on the coast to purchase much larger acreage in the state's interior, and by the 1950s the Sacramento Valley was rapidly gaining on the Santa Clara Valley in fruit production. In the 1960s it became apparent that everything had moved northeastward, and the time seemed right for Sunsweet to consolidate all of its operations into a single, modern, highly efficient plant. With fruit production shifting to the Sacramento Valley area, Yuba City became the logical choice for the new location.

By the early 1970s, after years of careful planning, construction of the plant was under way. To reduce costs, usable equipment from the older plants was salvaged and incorporated into the Yuba City facility, while outdated equipment and plants were sold to further defray costs. But the new facility did more than just reduce production costs; it provided the cooperative with an opportunity to expand into new areas of operations. One of these new endeavors was juice processing, added in 1976, enabling Sunsweet to have complete control over prune juice manufacture and distribution.

The 1980s have witnessed one of the most successful periods in the history of this industry—an era that Jackson characterizes as offering "growing opportunities." Today's health-conscious consumers have heightened the popularity of high-fiber Sunsweet prunes and other dried fruits; overseas, industrywide advertising was given a $4-million boost to promote the 1986 crop and $4.5 million for the 1987 crop through the Federal Targeted Export Assistance program, which provides funding for brand advertising.

Proud of its past and confident of its future, Sunsweet Growers Inc. looks forward to continuing and expanding its contribution to the prosperity of the Yuba/Sutter community and the whole of California.

The Sunsweet Growers Inc. plant, located at 901 North Walton Avenue, was built in 1975 and contains operations for processing and packing prunes and other fruit, and producing and bottling prune and cranberry juice.

PACIFIC GAS & ELECTRIC

In 1896 a project was started on the Yuba River system that would usher in a new era and dramatically change the way people lived, worked, and traveled.

Eugene DeSabla, John Martin, and Romulus Riggs Colgate, grandson of the famous soap company founder, combined efforts in a bold venture to produce hydroelectric power. They built the Rome Powerhouse in Nevada County to provide electrical service to the mining areas of Nevada City and Grass Valley. This venture was the beginning of what would eventually lead to the creation of the largest gas and electric company in the nation—Pacific Gas & Electric.

Incorporated in October 1897 as the Yuba Power Company, the business then proceeded to use the existing hydraulic mining water system, which flowed into Browns Valley, and built Yuba Power House. On March 21, 1898, electricity was supplied to the Browns Valley mines and transported 18 miles away to Marysville, primarily for commercial use. The first large customers of electricity in Marysville were the Buckeye Flour Mill, later bought out by Sperry, and the woolen mills. There was little market then for home use, so the backers looked to other areas for sale of their product.

Opportunity came in the form of a drought during 1897-1898. The Folsom powerhouse provided electricity for the Sacramento Street Railway system, but a diminishing water supply was making it difficult to keep the cars running. Recognizing an opportunity, John Martin, with characteristic daring, negotiated with Sacramento Electric Gas and Railway, and got a contract to deliver 2,200 kilowatts of electrical power for use in Sacramento. One-third of that supply was to be transmitted by September 1 of that same year.

This was the largest undertak-

The Colgate Powerhouse, constructed by the Yuba Electric Power Company in 1899 and expanded by Bay Counties Power Company in 1901.

ing Martin and his associates had ever attempted—the construction of the world-famous Colgate Power House on the Yuba River near Dobbins. Despite rockslides, arduous transportation over steep roads, and delays in flume construction, the job was completed on September 4, 1899, and power flowed into the street railway motors of Sacramento the following day—40,000 volts carried 61 miles. It was the highest transmission voltage in history.

Suddenly a new market appeared in the City of Oakland, the Oakland Transit Company. The Bay Counties Power Company was then formed by consolidating the Nevada and Yuba County projects. This company expanded the Colgate facility, and in 1901 power was transmitted 142 miles to Oakland—a new world record for distance and voltage. This linking of water power of the Sierras with the cities on the coast set the stage for the birth of a new industry.

Marysville had become the third city in California to have gas lighting in 1858, when pioneer businessman David E. Knight established the Marysville Coal Gas Com-

pany. The coal used to produce the gas was shipped from faraway places like Australia. By 1887 Knight's company began producing electricity from a crude generator. He formed the Marysville Gas and Electric Company in 1895.

The Bay Counties group decided to go into the retail distribution business and organized a new company—the California Central Gas and Electric Company. This company acquired the Marysville Gas and Electric Company and numerous other gas and electric distribution companies in Northern California.

Bay Counties and California Central then merged to become California Gas and Electric with Romulus Riggs Colgate as president. This firm acquired and gained control of nearly all the electric systems in Northern and Central California with the exception of the San Francisco Bay Area. Finally, in 1905, California Gas and Electric merged with San Francisco Gas and Electric to form what is now Pacific Gas and Electric Company.

Invention of the Pelton water wheel during that expansive period was crucial in the development of hydroelectric power. In fact, the whole hydroelectric field came into being with the invention of Lester Pelton—a gold miner turned carpenter who invented the wheel at

Camptonville in Yuba County.

Hydraulic mining and dredging, assisted by electrical power, retrieved from the Yuba River the greatest lode of gold of any stream in the United States, but the treacherous river also produced major flooding in the valley.

The floods in 1950 at Hammonton and in 1955 at Yuba City led to the creation of the Yuba County Water Agency in 1959. A major project was developed that resulted in construction of the New Bullards Bar Dam.

Most officials considered the project impossible for Yuba County, but the project was finally realized in 1970. It was the largest single construction contract of its kind in the United States.

PG&E agreed to sell its hydroelectric rights on the Yuba River to the agency and to purchase all power from this new project. The new Bullards Bar Dam now provides significant flood protection and a reliable irrigation water supply at essentially no cost to the local citizens. The long-term agreement with PG&E has made this possible.

PG&E continued to manufacture gas from coal until the 1940s. This changed when, in 1939, the Buttes Gas and Oil Company developed natural gas production in the Sutter Buttes area. The area straddling the Sacramento River from Princeton to Grimes has since become a major gas production area, with nearly 500 producing wells. PG&E purchases this natural gas and brings it into its system through a 400-mile network of collection lines in the Colusa-Sutter area.

When John Martin ran an electrical line to the Onstott ranch in Yuba City in 1898, it changed the history of farming in California. The Onstott ranch was the location of the first electrically operated pump for irrigation water in the state. Soon canneries and processing

plants had increased capability with electrical power, and by 1920 a system of electrically powered railroads, operated throughout the valley as far north as Red Bluff, made shipping of crops much more effi-

Gasworks of the Marysville Coal Gas Company were established in 1858 at Second and B streets.

cient. Modernization helped Yuba and Sutter counties become major agricultural suppliers in the state.

The history of Yuba and Sutter counties is entwined with the history of PG&E, and it has proved to be a real partnership in progress.

The Buttes Gas and Oil Company developed natural gas wells in 1939 in Sutter County, and PG&E contracted to purchase the gas production.

LIVE OAK BUILDING SUPPLY, INC.

Tommie Melton's meteoric rise in the fiercely competitive construction business began when he was still a teenager working with his father, Tom, building homes in Live Oak.

When his father retired, Tommie secured his contractor's license, hired a crew of three men, and started his own company. Young as he was, he knew all phases of building. As the job demanded, he was architect, planner, engineer, builder, and mason—always with an eye for the perfection that

Tommie G. Melton, founder of Melton & Melton Construction, purchased Live Oak Building Supply in the 1960s and used it to provide construction material for this building venture. Melton, active in the community, was a city councilman, reserve police officer, and one of the youngest mayors in Live Oak's history.

produces quality. As a result, his reputation for fine workmanship, reliability, and honesty spread, and the business grew rapidly.

Melton soon purchased the Live Oak Building Supply Co. in Live Oak, and hired a manager and three employees to run the business. He then purchased supplies for Melton & Melton Construction from this firm.

In 1967 he again expanded—this time into development. He built a portion of the area known as Southland Village, where his quality, custom homes further established him as a top contractor.

His next project, in partnership with Skip Morrison, was the purchase of 30 acres in South Yuba City, 10 acres of which was developed into 30 lots known as Teesdale Subdivision Unit #1. He bought out Morrison's interest, and in 1973 built 30 homes on that land, 26 of which were customized. In 1975 he developed the adjacent 20 acres, Teesdale Subdivision Unit #2, and began building two years later. It was completed in 1980 with another 69 homes being built.

In 1979 he purchased land at the edge of Live Oak, near Highway 99, and started construction of a new building and lumberyard for Live Oak Building Supply, which had been incorporated in 1972. The work was subcontracted for the most part (as Melton was busy developing another subdivision), and the new store was completed in July 1980.

The new project, Forestwood Estates, north of Yuba City, consisted of duplexes, triplexes, fourplexes, apartment buildings, and single-family residences.

The venture was speculative, and sales were slow for the next two years, during which time real estate in the area was in a slump. An uptrend in the market occurred in 1983, and sales began to increase.

Kathleen Melton assumed active management of the two companies, Live Oak Building Supply and Melton & Melton Construction following the death of her husband in 1986.

Melton was active in community affairs and was a city councilman, a reserve police officer, and one of the youngest mayors in Live Oak's history. He belonged to the Yuba/Sutter Builder's Association, and served on the board of North State Title Company.

His death in December 1986 left a complex business legacy. His wife, Kathleen Melton, has displayed remarkable business acumen and a determination to continue the work begun by her husband. Today she successfully heads the companies her husband founded, with son David as one of the contractors, and daughter Karen Vines working in the main office in Live Oak.

LAMON CONSTRUCTION CO., INC.

Lamon Construction is a family-owned business that has grown into one of Northern California's leading builders.

The company was started in 1950 by Lonnie Lamon, who had been a construction foreman in the Yuba/Sutter area for more than 25 years. It was a one-man, bid-on-anything business.

When Lamon died in 1952 his three sons took over management of the firm. Because of their respective jobs and schooling the brothers lived in different parts of the state. But strong family ties and deep roots in Sutter County persuaded them to continue the work started by their father.

They made a good team. Grady, the oldest, and a registered engineer, became president. He and W.H. "Henry" shared responsibility in the field. John, the youngest, joined the firm in 1956 after graduating with an engineering degree from the University of California, Berkeley. He became secretary/treasurer and managed the office and yard.

The Lamon brothers built the company into a large operation by avoiding the intensely competitive home-building business, concentrating instead on commercial and public buildings—a field in which they excelled.

Many of the projects performed by Lamon Construction are nonbid, negotiated jobs, for which the company handles all facets—from preliminary plans to owner acceptance of the completed building.

The firm builds throughout California; in the Yuba/Sutter area alone it is responsible for more than 100 structures. These public and commercial buildings are an eloquent testimonial to the fine reputation for craftsmanship and integrity the Lamon organization has earned through the years.

Yuba City offers fine examples of the quality projects the brothers have completed. One is a sleek, low-silhouette, 5,000-square-foot addition to the nineteenth-century county courthouse, virtually doubling the county's office space.

Another striking example is the American Savings building on Plumas Street. This unique structure is famous for a reason that is never perceived by the hundreds of people who pass it each day: It is the first building in the United States to have a concrete roof poured with "shrinkage-compensating" cement. This revolutionary product was developed by T.Y. Lin & Associates, and is used by Lamon because tests showed it cured without cracking and required no coating of any kind to seal off moisture.

Among other projects are a traditional European-style Serbian Orthodox Church in Carmichael and the modern, functional St. Isador's Catholic Church in Yuba City.

The brothers have been active participants in community and civic

The Lamon brothers continued the business their father founded in 1950. Shown (left to right): Henry, Grady, and John Lamon, in a photo taken in the late 1950s.

affairs, Grady having served as mayor of Marysville, and Henry as mayor of Yuba City. The company has received many awards for public service and excellence throughout the years.

When Grady died in 1985, John and Henry continued the company's tradition of quality and integrity started by their father nearly 40 years ago.

An example of one of the many commercial projects undertaken by Lamon Construction Co. is this modern Appeal Democratic Newspaper building erected in 1986.

KUBA & KXEZ RADIO

KUBA Radio is a contemporary country music station that also provides the largest broadcast news service coverage in the Yuba-Sutter area. Listeners are kept informed on local news by two professionals, and nationally from the extensive services of United Press International high-speed wire service and radio network. KXEZ-FM programs light rock music.

Throughout its 40-year history, which has seen many changes, KUBA has steadily grown. The success of the station reflects good management, innovative broadcasting, and community service.

KUBA Radio went on the air as an independent, non-network affiliated AM radio station in January 1948. It had a 500-watt unlimited operation of 1,600 kilocycles, and was located at 1479 Sanborn Road on the outskirts of Yuba City. It was founded by five equal partners: Beverly "Bud" Ballard, Clyde Goodnight, Chester Ullum, Dewey Allred, Jr., and Raymond F. Kinn. Ballard served as general manager, Goodnight as commercial manager, and Ullum as chief engineer.

A new corporation was formed in 1949 by three of the original

The KUBA Mobile Unit broadcasts annually from the Yuba-Sutter Fair.

partners—Ullum, Goodnight, and Allred. Also at that time a new multitower directional antenna system was installed, which boosted daytime power to 1,000 watts. The studio was moved to the Marysville Hotel in downtown Marysville, but the transmitter and power system remained in Yuba City.

Roger R. Hunt became station manager in 1950, the same year that KUBA joined the Dallas-based Lib-

KUBA's entry in the annual Easter Seals' Chili Cookoff.

erty Broadcasting network. When Liberty folded in 1952, KUBA again became independent.

In the late 1940s Ric Young was program director for KUBA. She is reputed to be the first female program director in the United States. Lon Simmons is another celebrity who started his career at KUBA. Simmons, who is known as the voice of the Oakland A's baseball team, worked at KUBA, broadcasting local high school sporting events.

Reorganization in 1954 made the station a partnership with Chet Ullum and Roger Hunt. Ullum was president and Hunt the general manager.

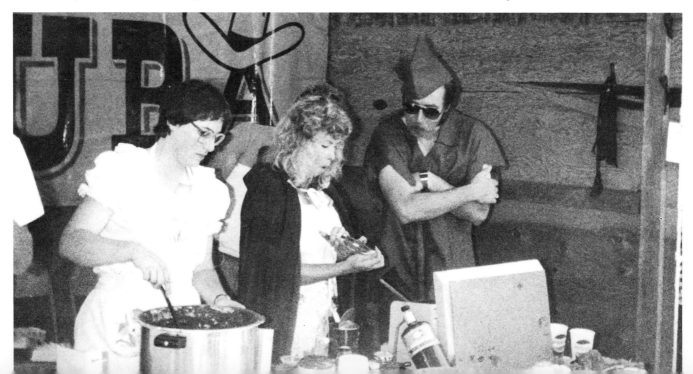

Daytime power was increased again in 1959, to 5,000 watts, and the station operated daily from 5 a.m. to midnight. In 1963 studios were moved from the Marysville Hotel to the Hart Building in downtown Marysville.

Sidney and Della Grayson, as Grayson Broadcasting, purchased the station in June 1965. Sidney Grayson served as president and general manager until 1967, when he appointed Bob Cain as general manager. In 1969 Cain became commercial manager and Stu Klein general manager.

The Marysville studio was moved to Yuba City in the 1970s, and since that time all station operations have emanated from the Yuba City transmitting site on Sanborn Road.

The station was sold again in 1971, to Cascade Broadcasting Co., with David Jack as president and Gary W. Gregory general manager. At that time the station adopted a contemporary music format. In 1973 KUBA joined ABC Entertainment Network. The FM station KHEX, with 3,000 watts of power, was added in 1974.

Leroy Neider and Eugene Mills bought the station in 1976; they changed the format to country music. Mel Peterson managed the stations from 1976 to 1982. The call letters were changed to KXEZ in 1978.

The present owner of KUBA/KXEZ is Ridge L. Harlan, who purchased the stations in January 1983. His son, Robert Harlan, is general manager. They kept the country music format on KUBA, but changed the FM station format to light rock music in 1983.

KUBA has come a long way since it began in 1948. It now has a staff of 25 employees, and is the primary broadcast advertising source in the Yuba-Sutter area. Facilities continue to expand to meet the growing needs of the community.

Community service is a priority with KUBA, and that service was of the highest order during the catastrophic flood of 1986. KUBA immediately went into 24-hour emergency broadcasting on a noncommercial basis. It was the primary source of information in the area during that dangerous period, and it is safe to say that most households in the area had their radio dials set at 1600 KUBA.

In recognition for "exceptional achievement" in the field of emergency broadcasting, KUBA was honored at a special dinner in Foster City, and presented an Outstanding Service Award for its efforts during the flood by the California Emergency Services Association.

KUBA was also honored for its service during the devastating flood of 1955. It remained on the air until 3.5 feet of water finally forced closure of the facility at Yuba City for three days.

Since its inception more than 40 years ago KUBA has strived to serve the whole community. On Sundays two foreign language programs are presented on KXEZ-FM. From 5 a.m. to 8 a.m. Hector Gomez hosts a Spanish-language program that was started more than two decades ago by Frank Meija. From 7 p.m. to 11 p.m. a program in Punjabi is conducted by Nirmal Shergill and Harbhajan Johl, who originated the program in 1968. Both programs feature native music, news, and community events.

Each year KUBA, in conjunction with Yuba City Park and Recreation, sponsors a special Holloween Party at Cal Skate that draws some 1,500 children. KUBA also sponsors a community Easter Egg Hunt at the fairgrounds each year.

General manager Robert Harlan is an active community leader. He is president of Easter Seals Society and was chairman for that organization's fund-raising event—the Chili Cookoff. He is also active in the chamber of commerce; in 1989 he will be president of the chamber. He has also served as a committee member of the California Prune Festival, which began its first year in September 1988.

The staff of KUBA & KXEZ Radio.

CONTINENTAL CABLEVISION

Cable television is one of the fastest-growing industries in twentieth-century America. From its early days in the 1950s, when it served as a community antenna in rural areas, to its present role of providing a wide selection of entertainment and information services in both rural and urban areas, cable television has become part of American life.

Continental Cablevision, serving the Yuba/Sutter area, began in 1963 in response to the initial challenge of providing better television reception for two small Ohio communities. With an abundance of entrepreneurial spirit and a modest investment, the company was formed and received a 20-year franchise from the towns of Tiffin and Fostoria in Ohio. The following year Edward and Joyce Ageter of Tiffin became Continental's first subscribers. They remain subscribers today.

Continental has experienced exceptional growth since that first installation, now serving 1.5 million subscribers in more than 300 communities. Privately held by approximately 100 individuals and institutions, it is free from the pressures that often affect publicly traded companies.

"Our performance is built on

Continental Cablevision's new business office and local production facility at 311 B Street in Yuba County.

three principles to which we have closely adhered: First, we have carefully focused our efforts, limiting ourselves to those things we can do well. Second, we have built an organization that minimizes bureaucracy and emphasizes local autonomy. And third, we have worked hard to attract and retain talented and motivated people," says Amos B. Hostetter, chairman and chief executive officer.

Continental has become one of the most respected and financially secure cable companies. In

Customers visiting the newly renovated office receive fast and courteous service.

the fall of 1986, in the "Salute To Excellence" issue of *Channels,* a widely read communications magazine, Continental was recognized as "the best cable systems operator in the United States."

From the beginning the firm, headquartered in Boston, Massachusetts, has stressed quality, integrity, and long-term results. Since its inception it has been decentralized, giving its managers more local operation autonomy than any other company in the industry. Continental, also recognizes that community needs are best met by locally responsive management, and works hard to attract and keep talented, motivated people. Two-thirds of Continental's managers began in entry-level positions, and progressed through the ranks.

The firm's more than 3,000 employees receive ongoing training. For more than 10 years programs have been offered to technical and office personnel to help improve interdepartmental communications and to enhance customer services.

In October 1986 Continental assumed the cable operation in the Yuba/Sutter area, to where local manager John Pezzini, who has

Continental Cablevision's well-organized receiving and distribution center in Marysville.

been with Continental seven years, transferred from the Stockton office.

One of the first projects on his agenda for improving the system within the area was to conduct three extensive customer research surveys. Information received from the subscribers was then cross-tabulated, analyzed, and used for planning and decisions. It also enabled Pezzini to determine problem areas, and to begin a vast improvement of the whole system. Now cable lines are swept regularly to determine any problem spots, and maintenance is ongoing to assure good reception at all times.

Another area found to be in need of improvement was the business office's customer contact department. A complete renovation was mounted, and a new, computerized, high-capacity ROLM telephone system was installed to provide better service.

Basic service was expanded to 29 channels, and addressable convertors were installed to allow simple on-and-off service for premium programming. Previously, custom-

ers had to bring the boxes into the office for manual adjustment.

Survey results also indicated a need for program changes. Unpopular channels were dropped, and new ones added to the basic menu. WTBS/Atlanta, the most popular program choice with local subscribers, was added, along with Nickelodeon, a superior children's programming network that parents had requested. The Arts and Entertainment channel was selected, as was the popular C-Span, which transmits live coverage from the House of Representatives.

Continental maintains a community service television studio and a truck equipped to cover local events. Channel 5, the local station, presents a variety of programming and coverage, including the Bob Kai parade, and live-performance tapes from the Yuba/Sutter Fair, Beale Air Force Base Appreciation Days, and even the Wheatland Pet Parade.

Weekly programs include "Artists Alive," co-produced with the Yuba/Sutter Regional Arts Council; "Take 5," a local interview program; and "Community Reports," among others.

The cable company also is active in community events, such as the Toys For Tots drive at Christmas and, with the Yuba/Sutter Fair, co-sponsored a trip to Disneyland.

"Because we're sensitive to specific community needs," says John Pezzini, "we are now readying an Emergency Override System to be used in cooperation with cities and counties during an emergency situation, such as the flood in 1986."

Future plans include expanded channel capacity via the Scientific Atlanta Convertor. This will allow more basic channels to be added to the system, thereby continuing to integrate and upgrade facilities and services, and further participation in community affairs.

Technical services are available at no charge, and always within 24 hours.

CENTURY 21 SELECT REAL ESTATE INC.

Daniel Jacuzzi's grandfather would be proud of him.

When Daniel Jacuzzi bought Century 21 Real Estate from his father in 1980, he was only 24 years old, but was already an experienced businessman who was showing a strong bent for entrepreneurial enterprise. Jacuzzi had gone to work in the real estate field shortly after graduating from Yuba City High School in 1974. After two years he formed his own company—D.C. Jacuzzi Development—a firm that built houses in Yuba City, Sutter, and Browns Valley.

His father, Daniele Jacuzzi, opened his first Century 21 office on Gray Avenue in Yuba City in 1975—one of the first in Northern California. It began as a small one-agent business, but grew rapidly. When young Jacuzzi bought the business, there were eight agents, two secretaries, and two offices—in Yuba City, at 1224 Bridge Street, and in Marysville, at 615-10th Street, where both are still located today.

Jacuzzi not only expanded the business of the real estate offices, but expanded into other fields. In 1983 he opened a property man-

agement firm, which now manages more than 650 condominiums, apartments, and houses, and the following year formed a property maintenance company. In 1986 he founded the Select School of Real Estate—the first and only certified school in the area. Offering courses in real estate principles and pre-license training, the school is certified by the California Department of Education and approved by the Department of Real Estate. Jacuzzi has also become a certified instructor.

Jacuzzi incorporated the company in 1987, and hired a CPA to head the accounting department. Since Jacuzzi purchased it in 1980, Century 21 has grown to be the largest full-service real estate company in the area, and now has a staff of more than 40 employees in four separate offices.

He believes that his advertising slogan sums up his formula for success: "It's not being the biggest that makes you the best. It's being the best that makes you the biggest." Being the best means doing the best-possible job for your clients, and in many instances that involves innovative ideas. Jacuzzi has taken almost anything in trade, arranged tax-free exchanges, taken notes, assisted Cambodian refugee families to purchase businesses all over California and even loaned clients money to help them buy a

home.

Jacuzzi is proud of his company's innovation, stating that "if anyone can put together a sale, we can."

Success is not unusual in the Jacuzzi family. Their history reads like an American success story. His grandfather, Gelindo Jacuzzi, along with 13 brothers and sisters, immigrated from Italy between 1910 and 1920 and started an airplane company—Jacuzzi Brothers. After one of the brothers was killed in a tragic plane crash, they sold their design to Ryan Aircraft Co., which later used the basic design in building the famous *Spirit of St. Louis*—the airplane Charles Lindbergh flew across the Atlantic in 1927.

The brothers then started a water pump company. They invented a therapy device for one of the young children who suffered from rheumatoid arthritis—the Jacuzzi Spa, now world famous.

Daniel Jacuzzi's Century 21 Select Real Estate Inc. has come a long way since 1980, but this is really just the beginning of the story—growth and expansion will continue for many years.

Daniel Jacuzzi, owner of Century 21 Select Real Estate Inc.

The Jacuzzi Cabin Monoplane, a 1920 model 200-h.p. aircraft that carried six passengers and flew at 100 miles per hour, was developed by the Jacuzzi brothers. Gelindo Jacuzzi, one of the brothers, was Daniel Jacuzzi's grandfather.

PATRONS

The following individuals, companies, and organizations have made a valuable commitment to the quality of this publication. Windsor Publications and the Yuba/Sutter Regional Arts Council gratefully acknowledge their participation in *Changes in Harmony: An Illustrated History of Yuba and Sutter Counties.*

All West Aviation, Inc.
Ashby & Doughty, A Professional Law
    Corporation
E.I. Brandt Trucking Co., Inc.
Brown's Gas Company
Century 21 Select Real Estate Inc.*
Community Memorial Museum of Sutter
    County
Continental Cablevision*
Feather River Mills, Inc.
Thomas Frey Family
Dale L. Green, Inc.
Harkey House, Bed & Breakfast
Terrence L. Hoffer, M.D., Ph.D.
Huntley-Sheehy Insurance Co., Inc.*
International Turbo Center, Inc.
KUBA & KXEZ Radio*
Lamon Construction Co., Inc.*
Bob and Carol Lenhard
Lipp and Sullivan Mortuary Dan and Kay
    Gary, Owners
Live Oak Building Supply, Inc.*
City of Marysville
Marysville Joint Unified School District
Marysville Medical Group*
Marysville-Peikang Sister City Association
Meagher & Tomlinson Company,
    Commercial Real Estate Brokerage and
    Development
Ken Onstott
Pacific Gas & Electric*
Dr. Robert M. Peppercorn, M.D.*
Ed & Deanna Prothero d/b/a 7-Eleven
The Refuge
Dr. and Mrs. David L. Rozzen
Shamrock Realtors
Sunset Moulding Co., Inc.*
Sunsweet Growers Inc.*
Sutter County Free Library
Sutter County Superintendent of Schools
Valley View Packing Co., Inc.
Stephen White
The Wild Rice Exchange
Yuba City Scrap & Steel Inc.
Yuba City Unified School District
Yuba Community College District*
Yuba County Airport and Industrial
    Development Department
Yuba-Sutter Disposal, Inc.

*Partners in Progress of *Changes in Harmony: An Illustrated History of Yuba and Sutter Counties.* The histories of these companies and organizations appear in Chapter 7, beginning on page 103.

FOR
FURTHER
READING

Attrocchi, Julia C. *The Old California Trail.* Caldwell, Idaho: Caxton Printers, Ltd., 1945.

Bagley, Harry P. "A Woman's Tale of the Gold Rush." *The Sacramento Bee,* April 25, 1942.

Bates, D.B. *Incidents on Land and Water of Four Years on the Pacific Coast.* Boston: French & Co., 1857.

Bird, Jessica. *Appeal-Democrat 1960 Centennial Edition* 68: 1 (January 23, 1960).

Clark, Douglas M. *Wheatland Hop Field Riot.* M.A. thesis. California State University at Chico, 1963.

Coy, Owen C. *The Great Trek.* Los Angeles: Powell Publishing Co., 1931.

Delay, Peter J. *History of Yuba and Sutter Counties.* Los Angeles: Historic Record Co., 1924.

Ellis, W.T. *Memories: My Seventy-Two Years in the Romantic County of Yuba, California.* Eugene, Ore.: Nash, 1939.

Field, Stephen J. *Early Days in California.* New York: Da Capo, 1968.

George, Vivienne L. *Yuba City/Marysville, California.* Northridge, Calif.: Windsor Publications, 1980.

Gibbons, Boyd. "Oregon Trail: The Itch to Move West." *National Geographic Magazine* 170: 2 (August 1986).

Grun, Bernard. *1901-1972: The Timetables of History.* New York: Simon & Schuster, 1946.

Gudden, Erwin G., ed. *The Memoirs of Theodor Cordua: The Pioneer of New Mecklenburg in the Sacramento Valley.* San Francisco: California Historical Society, 1933.

Hague, Harlan. "The Reluctant Retirement of Thomas O. Larkin." *California History* 62: 1 (Spring 1983).

Heizer, Robert F., ed. *Handbook of North American Indians.* Vol. 8. Washington, D.C.: Smithsonian Institution, 1978.

Hendrix, Louise B. *Sutter Buttes: Land of Histum Yani.* Marysville, Calif.: Normart, 1981.

Hust, Stephen G. *This Is My Own, My Native Land.* Yuba City, Calif.: Independent Press, 1956.

Lague, Jim. *Gold Mountain Record Stories.* Vol. 3. Brownsville, Calif.: Yuba-Feather Historical Association, Inc., 1981.

Laney, Anita, ed. *Marysville: An Historical Sampler.* Marysville, Calif.: privately published (no date).

Lewis, Oscar. *Sutter's Fort.* New Jersey: Prentice Hall, 1966.

McGlashan, C.F. *History of the Donner Party.* Fresno, Calif.: California History Books, 1973.

McGowan, Joseph A. *History of the Sacramento Valley.* New York: Lewis Historical Pub., 1961.

McGowan, Joseph A. and Terry R. Willis. *Sacramento: Heart of the Golden State.* Northridge, Calif.: Windsor Publications, 1983.

Magee, David. *California's Pictorial Letter Sheets: 1849-1869.* San Francisco, 1967.

Morowitz, Harold J. *Cosmic Joy and Local Pain.* New York: Scribner's, 1987.

Mossinger, Rosemarie. *Woodleaf Legacy.* Colorado Springs, Col.: Young Life, 1975.

Murphy, Virginia R. *Across the Plains in the Donner Party.* Olympic Valley, Calif.: Outbooks, 1977.

Olmstead, R.R. *Scenes of Wonder and Curiosity.* Berkeley, Calif.: Howell North, 1962.

Pahl, Nikki, Mary Swisher, and Genevieve Troka. *Camera Craft.* Sacramento: Sacramento History Center, 1982.

Pennoyer, A. Sheldon, ed. *This Was California, A Collection of Woodcuts and Engravings.* New York: Putnam's, 1938.

Powell, J.W., ed. *North American Ethnology.* Vol. 3. Washington, D.C.: Government Printing, 1877.

Powers, Stephen. *California Indian Characteristics and Centennial Mission to the Indians of Western Nevada and California.* Berkeley, Calif.: Bancroft Library, 1975.

Ramey, Earl. *The Beginnings of Marysville.* San Francisco: California Historical Society, 1936.

_____. *The History of Yuba County.* The Yuba County Historical Commission, 1976.

Rawls, James J. "Great Expectations." *California History* 61: 3 (1982).

Scherer, James A.B. *The First Forty-Niner.* New York: Minton, Balch & Co., 1925.

Silverstein, Shel. *Where the Sidewalk Ends.* New York: Harper and Row, 1974.

Smith, Alson J. *Men Against the Mountains: Jedediah Smith.* New York: John Day Co., 1965.

Watkins, T.H. *California: An Illustrated History.* Palo Alto, Calif.: American West, 1973.

Wheat, Carl I., ed. *The Shirley Letters: From the California Mines 1851-1852.* New York: Ballantine, 1971.

Wilkes, Charles. *Exploring Expedition.* Vol. 5. Philadelphia: Lea and Blanchard, 1845.

Williams, C.E. *Yuba and Sutter Counties, California: Their Resources, Advantages and Opportunities.* San Francisco: Bacon, 1887.

Workman, Lottie L. *Hammonton "Dredger Town," 1902-1957.* Marysville, Calif.: 1968.

Yuba County Historical Commission. *Bicentennial: 1776-1976.* Marysville, Calif.: 1976.

Zollinger, James P. *Sutter.* New York: Oxford, 1939.

Facing Page: Skagg's Safeway store at 421 D Street in Marysville sold cans of gulf shrimp at two for 25 cents, and large-sized loganberries for 69 cents in 1930. Courtesy, California State Library

INDEX